How To Quit Your Job, and do it well!

A real-world guide to leaving your job and living a great life, doing things you like to do

by Matt Wright

For my two favourite L's

Step One:

Resign with enough time left to work your notice period.

Contents

Part I: Review

Introduction	4
Chapter 1 – The base beliefs	17
Chapter 2 – Behaving like a hamster	32
Chapter 3 – The hurdles	44
1. The Fear Factor	45
2. Everyone else can't be wrong…right?	56
3. Timing	69
4. What if I 'fail'?	77
5. Pay cheque addiction	83
6. Past Investment and Sacrifice	91
Summary	100
Chapter 4. So what do I do now……?	103

Part II: Activation

Introduction	112
Chapter 5: Financial planning and readiness	119
Chapter 6. What you *love* vs what you can *do*	135
Chapter 7. Understanding there is no fixed format – my example	143
Chapter 8. Take control	153
Chapter 9. Entering your chosen market	163
Chapter 10. JFDI!	175
Chapter 11. Reality Checks	183
Chapter 12. What's setting out on your own / going solo actually like?	193
Chapter 13. What if you just don't do it?	201

Part I: Review

Introduction

I am very much what I would call a 'regular' normal person. Furthermore, I'm introverted, I suffer anxiety, and I tend to socialise within a small group of friends. I often struggle when meeting new people, and am awkward in new situations. However, I found the courage to quit a well-paid job just over five years ago working as a senior manager in a huge organisation and have never looked back. I have since also not had another job. I now live my life in a completely different, fulfilling, and self-sustaining way. You could say I that have done what many consider as the bravest thing a middle aged 'successful' person can do, despite the barriers I had before me. I literally just decided I had had enough and was determined to do things differently. So, this is why I'm here. To tell you about this journey and try and give you the tools and the courage to see if you can (and want to) do the same. I hope, for some of you at least, what you will be able to learn from me will change your life forever in ways you can simply not comprehend at the moment. I know how much my life has changed for the better in the last few years, and how I would have never seen myself in this position. I really wish for this to happen for you too.

'How to quit work well'. This title took barely a few seconds to come up with when I decided to write this book, because it was all I had been thinking about for some time in my 'previous' life. How *do* I quit work? And how *do* I do it well? The title though has really been the easy bit. The tough bit is I am a complete stranger to you. I have to convince you that I've done this, and that I have done it well! I also need to convince you that I am simply just a regular person and not some anomaly, so you feel you can also make the same changes I have made. I will do my very best to do this in the coming pages, but first let's outline what 'quitting work well' really means. For me and I would suggest for most other people, it is several basic things:

Well….as in proudly and with dignity
Well….as in maintaining good physical and mental health
Well….as in living a good life and providing for myself and/or my family

So, having done it, five years have now gone by and the best bit of news is that I'm still here…. I'm not homeless ….my wife didn't leave me (yet!) …..and I'm happier than ever. I *did* quit work with dignity. I have *vastly* improved both my mental and physical health, and I have furthermore now grown *beyond* my financial ability to provide for my family, compared to when I had my job.

While writing this right now, I am sat at the back of my house (the same one I owned when I had a job), working on this book on my computer, in my home office. In the last five years I have had many truly great experiences, and now have many new skills under my belt that I have learnt in this period, enjoying a varied and fulfilling life. I know I take for granted sometimes what I have accomplished and how different life is for me and, perhaps more importantly, for my whole family now. And don't get me wrong, by different I mean unfathomably better. I almost can't comprehend what my life was like before, even though it was only a few years ago. I drop my son off at school and pick him up *every* day without the worry of being late for work or missing an 'important' meeting. I spend much more time with my wife, my parents and my small group of friends. I cherish my relationships so much more, and I hope am a much nicer and better person to be around. It's amazing to me now when I look back, how you never realise how all-consuming a so called 9-5 job is. Certainly, for those of us who have reached middle age and have reached some degree of apparent 'success'. It is barely ever really 9-5, it impregnates all aspects of our lives and relationships. Many, many people find themselves in terrible situations, where they work all hours against unmanageable deadlines. Work encroaches far into their personal life, physical, and mental well-being. That's why I decided it would be crucial for me to try and analyse my successes and failures, and provide some good advice to help others. Those, who like me, just never got on well with what I would loosely call 'the norm' of salaried employment. I'm not talking about 'work' (I work very hard, even harder now than I ever did). Nor am I suggesting you or I are someone who is lazy or unmotivated. I'm talking about not having a healthy relationship with paid employment. At points in my life, as I'm sure you have, I truly hated the idea of 'working a job' for a living. Even at its best it barely managed to float my boat at all, and was simply a way of providing a wage. I can honestly say I have never had a job that I 'loved'. What also became very apparent, was that as I entered what is traditionally labelled as 'midlife', my employment began to grate on me…a lot. The idea, as I became more and more traditionally successful in my career, that I would need to keep going and going well into my 60s or even 70s, really started to depress me significantly. I felt trapped…maybe even as far as calling myself truly lost. I simply mean I hated the idea of 'working' at my job. I had developed this so-called career, with specific skills and experience in a field I had no interest in. I had just stumbled in to it as many people do. I didn't someday wake up and decide I wanted to be a project manager (which was my career). The politics, the monotony, the personal sacrifice, the invasion it had on my life. The searching for scraps of evidence to warrant my yearly 'Met' mark on my management annual review. I found the whole experience hard work enough, let alone actually fulfilling the needs of the job itself. Sadly, what I have also found in my more recent life, is that there are so many more people out there that feel *exactly* the same way I did. I know of so many people who just feel trapped in a career they have unwittingly forged out for themselves and truly believe, as I did, that there is no way out. Yet, I am living proof that there is. I can promise you there are ways to change your life significantly and so much more for the better.

However, don't think that by my not 'working a job', I mean not working hard, or doing something useful with your life. I'm not here to sell you any passive income ideas, or get rich quick business plans. No. Like me, I've already told you, you will have to work hard, awfully hard to decide to quit your job. It is quite likely in fact you will need to work harder than you ever have before….but you can be enriched in a way you never felt possible. My own experience is one of the classic 'middle aged manager'. In reality this is who I originally was going to write this book for, but please don't think this opportunity is just for *some* people. The experiences and tools we will be discussing in this book are really adaptable to anyone at any point in their life, in any situation.

In this modern world I'm sure most of you will agree, that the majority of Society Class the ability to earn a higher monetary income, is the true measure of 'success'. I for one thought this to be true, well into my forties. However, from my new experiences, I can tell you know that it truly is not the case. I *feel* successful now. Outside of the balance of funds in my bank, I am able to measure myself differently now in so many other ways. Yes I have *also* gained some financial success, but it hasn't been like that for the whole last 5 years. Far from it, I have had to make many 'financial sacrifices' along the way (we will talk about this later in the book). Yet I have still had a fundamental feeling of success and gratitude, far greater than I had when I was in my job. Of course, many of the more 'Socially Successful' people *seem* happier and more in control of their lives because they are affluent. Yet, I can tell you, they will have many of the same concerns, worries and self-doubts as anyone else. Money does not make these people, you, or me any different or of any less *value* to themselves or others. Of course, often people are privileged, or lucky, or have great intelligence in specific fields, which gives them a greater chance of a larger monetary income. But fundamentally doing what I did and helping you to do the same, it matters not where you are starting from or the skills and experiences you have had. Each and every one of us has the capability to achieve and measure our own success in many ways. Furthermore, you are not limited financially by anything other than your own self-worth and belief in your own version of what success means.

I hope having seen the simple title I have given to this book, and now started to read it, you are able to understand yourself whether you are one of the people that fall into the same category as I do. I'm going to say that the fact you have bought this and/or are reading it based on the title means that you are looking for a different way of doing things. Perhaps you just need the right nudge, the right toolkit, or the right discussion with someone who knows about the journey and can support you to accomplish it too. Of course, it is not for everyone. Of the people I know who are struggling bitterly with working a traditional job, I also know many who have fantastic careers and vocations that they find truly fulfilling. This is wonderful, and we desperately need people like this; our passionate teachers, doctors, artists, builders, or even those that are happy just doing their regular job and going home to their family at the end of the day to sleep like a baby. In many ways, I was always incredibly jealous of those people. They have it made, they have it sorted, they are sitting pretty just cruising along, happy as can be. And good for them! There are ***many*** types of people, but I, and most likely you …are not one of those lucky people who are where they are supposed to be.

Now, in my time I have read many self-help books. There are some quite interesting ones too, although I won't cite any as they never ***really*** helped me enough to the extent that they gave me the incentive to make a change. I'm guessing this won't be your first self-help book either. The benefit for you though, is this isn't a self-help book. Not in the traditional sense anyway. I have never written professionally before so most definitely lack the ability to write a 'proper' book anyway. Therefore, instead, what I would like is for you to think of this more as a record of a conversation you and I are having. I'm going to use what I've done, what I've learned, everything I've experienced from my journey from having a job and career, to being self-sustainable, and try and help you to take the same journey yourself. I will package it in a way so you can take bite sized chunks, digest them, and then use it to help you make some very impactful decisions. I will provide no promise of fame and fortune, no instructions for a technology empire, or any of the other usual drivel that can drop out of the self-help/quit work genres ….. but what I will say is it will be just me and you, and an opportunity for you to create a wonderful and fulfilling life like I have created. One that I truly felt was impossible for the first years of my life.

What is not going to be in this book is a step-by-step guide to a specific outcome or role in your life. The whole principle of what I have done and what I am going to share with you is making things much more personal in your life. I don't know what you like, what impassions you, what you are good at. But I *do* know, from my own experience, how you can take ***practical steps*** and actions to utilise what you know about yourself to make those things more important in your life. I could write a very long list of the experiences I have had and things I have done in my journey since leaving my job, some of which I will use for you as examples as we progress. Yet the bottom line is it is *my* journey and the micro details are almost insignificant compared to me sharing the capabilities and mind set I required to make it happen. It makes no sense for someone to follow the exact same journey as I have…frankly I don't need the competition! You will all need to make it your own, and personalise your experience. I will however be your guide, and I will tell you *how* I have achieved it and what *you* need to do to do the same.

One of the most powerful things I believe I can say to you before we begin, is I can literally *guarantee* to you……. with my hand on heart, that five to ten years ago I would have had myself as the *least* likely person I knew to quit my job. I am very certain too that if I asked my long-term friends, they would also give a similar answer. I literally could never have imagined that after grafting for years, in my 40's, I would just gather my gear and leave a well-paid, stable job, to enter a world of change, uncertainty and self-sufficiency. I've already told you I'm an introvert, I can struggle socially, and I suffer from anxiety. Yet because I am aware of these issues and I also know how strongly I would have disbelieved that I could do it, I also know for a *fact*, that if its right for you, we can do the same for your life. We can explore the process and the journey together, answer the tough questions together and find out truly what ability and passion is hidden inside you. We can then mould it and nurture it, and you will be surprised what amazing things you will be able to accomplish. I will *promise* to be there for you for the whole journey through this book, and beyond if you wish. I will make myself accessible. (Details at the end of the book...never offer something you aren't willing to provide). As we continue this conversation, one vital thing to remember always is that I am just a normal everyday person. During my many conversations with people about my life, I nearly always get told that I must be different or 'special'. It always puts a smile on my face! I guarantee you I have no more skills, influence, talent, insight, knowledge, capability or potential than you do. I am unique yes, but so are you......yet we are also very much the same basic human being with the same fears and anxieties.

So, getting back to me five to ten years ago.... I was obsessed with promotion, with my outward persona, people's opinion of me.....I was (and still am at times) not confident in my capabilities. I suffered from the 'what if' syndrome. I had a huge chip on my shoulder, and frankly thought myself a bit of a victim of circumstance. I could go on for a whole page with reasons why life and the world was stacked against me and why I couldn't make a change. That being said I don't want to promise you the world however, it may not be for everyone. Not everyone has it in them, nor perhaps are able to create the right circumstances to make the jump...Don't forget, many people love their job and gain great satisfaction from life operating with the majority. I wish them all well and am thankful they have found their passion. As I said earlier, the fact you have picked this book up and are reading it tells me we have a really good probability set out before us that I can help you change your life, otherwise you wouldn't still be here in the first place, right? So please *do* get excited that we have found each other and please *do* open your mind to new ideas and possibilities as we start this journey.

From now on in, I am going to assume you are 'in' for the rest of this conversation and are convinced enough that I can help you achieve something you do actually desire, that is in fact the same, or very near to what I have achieved. I am going to converse with you on the basis that my experiences in making this change are where I get my authority to work with you to do the same. You don't really know me at all from reading a few pages about me, but what you *do* know (unless I'm a pathological liar), is quite simply.... I've done it. I have 'quit work well'! I've been a successful employee, hardworking, committed, yet I've managed to leave it all behind to find an alternative path, well into my adult life. I still maintain my health, my home and my past relationships. Well, most of my relationships anyway, but we will touch on this later as some people will find it difficult to accept the changes you make. I

have the experience; I have ***felt*** the feelings and I have ***lived*** the practicalities. I have learned much from doing it and have the opportunity to share this with you, and I am excited and humbled to do so. I genuinely hope that if even a few people could make such massive changes as I have from reading this book, that it will be worth the effort of putting these words to paper.

In a nutshell, my gift to you for buying this book is that I open up everything about me, showing you a journey that will, with hope, change your life beyond measure. I will do as much as I can to pass to you my experiences, emotions and knowledge of making the move, and together we will give you the best chance possible to know 'how to quit work well'. Come with me, it's time we kicked this off, because I don't know about you…but I can't wait to get going.

Chapter 1 – The base beliefs

I know I have been in the very lucky position to have successfully managed to make the jump away from paid employment. I have also had the privilege already of helping others to do the same, as I hope to do with you. Because of this experience, I have learnt there are three core realities that I believe you need to understand in order to have the greatest chance of success. Actually, I believe in them strongly enough to refer to them as ***three simple facts***.

Fact 1 - You are *no* different from me

Or more importantly, you need to realise that I am no different from you. Again, I don't mean everyone is the same, and we have already talked about making the journey your own, using your own skills and experiences etc. I simply mean that fundamentally you and I are just 'normal' people. I mean that despite everyone being individual, there is nothing different between us as human beings. For many years I did, however, think I was in some way 'special' (and I don't mean in a good way!). Like I did, you too may feel you are isolated or estranged from others at your place of work. Perhaps you also hate your job, you feel trapped, you long for more, for an alternative way of life, feeling fundamentally different from those around you. You believe you don't even think anything like your work colleges. You may even carry an outward persona. You may have an interesting Myers Briggs personality type. You may not understand why you are so unhappy, or why it is so difficult for you to be happy with your career or job. The absolute bottom line is, basically…you're not that different.

Nearly everyone, me included (for a long time), has, or has had at one point in their life some kind of significant entitlement problem. 'I should be paid more'……'I'm different from everyone else'……'I'm misunderstood'……'it's not fair'……'why can't it be ME that wins the lottery'……'why do I have to manage my bosses tasks at work'. Many people, particularly those that achieve some kind of apparent Social success in their (wrongly chosen) working career, suffer from the problem that they believe they are 'special'. It's the best way to describe it! Yes, it is normal to think we should be valued more, or we are wired differently from other people. Yet we also often believe that we are burdened in some way with bad luck, or poor relationships, or are victims of circumstance. Maybe everything is the fault of your crappy bosses. I was the absolute king of this. I thought *everyone* at work was out to get me, thought poorly of me and climbed all over me to get promoted. Despite having actually carved out a very successful career, I still felt hard done by and a failure, as well as the fact that everyone around me was surely feeling so much better. The reality is, it just simply wasn't true! This is just myself confusing the fact my mind and body were trying to tell me I was doing the wrong thing in the wrong place. And there are many, many more like ME!

It will hurt you, as it hurt me to realise, that this is the hard truth and you're maybe not so 'special', you just perhaps need to change your focus in life. It took me a long time to realise this. The 'differences' I saw were actually just self-fantasised excuses not to face the truth. Yes, there are always individualities, unique quirks, differences in experiences, skills, values and beliefs, and this is the beauty of what you can embrace when you make the change. Yet, one *huge* aspect that helped me realise I could do things differently, is that if you cut all the crap, the crusty exteriors, the facades, the excuses…all that makes up your *outward* being you present to the world, we are…..well, fundamentally all just a human, like anyone else. Furthermore, more likely than not, you are only feeling how you are feeling because your mind and body wants you to change, and you are just manifesting alternative reasons to ignore them.

At the time of writing this I have already told you I don't have a job. I have a Masters engineering degree from a red brick university, I have worked for several large corporations and government organisations and have had the 'privilege' of being in receipt of a significant remuneration package. Until I was 38 years old, I was looking at the stairs to corporate success. I had it all…Designer suits, a nice car, the ongoing stress over producing a report nobody would read, the anxiety of trying to meet an unreachable delivery target. Yet today, I sit here having this conversation with you, in combat trousers and a rather comfortable running top, looking out on my garden. I set my own agenda, my own goals, my own measure of achievement. You, however, I'm guessing are currently working a career, yes? So, you are where I was…which means you *can* be where I am now. Very soon it will be time to discuss with you whether you are both willing and able to make the shift in mindset and prepare to jump.

The first thing I learnt when I finally realised, I could jump the corporate ship, was this concept of mistaking this difference I felt to simply being an internal conversation I was ignoring. I still chuckle when I speak to parents at my child's school and they look at me in wonderment when I tell them I don't have a job. I can see it now, the look on their faces, as if I have the Holy Grail right there smugly tucked under my arm. Then the questions come…'How did you do it?'……'How do you afford to live?'……'What's the secret?'. Instantly there it is, someone thinking they are different from me, looking for the magic formula, the key, the secret. Desperately trying to grab that one special thing they have missed staring them right in the face. That sudden desperation that comes from within, hoping that I will take pity on them and make it all ok by telling them the half dozen magic words. And I don't. Why?

The fact is that the true secret, is that there isn't one. Just as there is no real 'get rich quick' scheme. Just as all those glossy pictures and videos from internet advertising gurus are only about getting money from you, not about giving you the 'true secret' to Network Marketing. There is no big secret…. anywhere. That is the secret! The secret is there isn't a secret!

'So, what on earth am I doing here then!" you say. Well, you are here to realise that that is the case! To understand that instead, there are just a number of practical things to think about and questions to answer. Then you too can master 'the secret'. The quicker you understand that you are no different (in principle) from the top-level executive running IBM, then the quicker we will get through this conversation. Do not be under the assumption the CEO of IBM is a 'better' human being than you, nor the poor guy you last saw on the street is some kind of degenerate. They are both normal human beings, like you and me. Ergo, Fact 1…. You are **no** different from me.

Fact 2 – you are not *'owed'* anything

Nobody and I mean **nobody**, owes you a living, is getting in your way, or has been given a 'better' start than you……. unless you have either let them, or you truly believe they have. You and you alone have the capacity to live out any scenario you wish, and it is entirely down to your attitude and hard graft. Fact. 'Oh what about those people who are born rich, or those that win the lottery, or that guy off that talent show that now travels the world singing?' you say. Yes…what about them? Have they had lucky breaks? Sure. Have they perhaps been born into a different scenario to you? Sure. Can they sing better than you!? Of course! Yet are there any fewer rich or famous people who are miserably unhappy, or horribly depressed with their lot in life? No, actually there are **many** rich and famous people who suffer with depression and anxiety because of the complexities of having anything and everything they think they want, and yet they still feel unfulfilled. Probably because like me, they realise none of that actually matters. Think of your own situation. Have you ever bought a new (to you) car, or tv, or saved up for some other expensive 'toy' to reward yourself for all the hard work you have done in your job? Felt great for a couple of days, right? Maybe even a few weeks or months. After that? It just becomes the norm. The new car is not new anymore. The new toy doesn't have the same gravitas to it. Once you have enough money to feed yourself, house yourself and cloth yourself and your family, the effect of money dwindles significantly and it makes little difference whatsoever. Rich people and poor people still have worries, self-doubt and fears.

Why should you spend one precious breath caring about what someone else has, or can do? Why for example do you care if the director of your section at work, or your shift manager, or anyone you know, apparently has it 'so much better than you'. It gives you ***nothing***, it helps you in no way. In fact, all it does is add fuel to the fires of envy, entrapment, depression and feelings that others are in some way better than you. This is also ***mostly*** simply down to the perception of money and how much someone may or may not have. Money and status should be consequential to what we do. They should never be the drivers behind what we do and who we are. They should be the ***product*** of what we do and who we are. The majority of people who are unhappy in their career fall into the camp of people that measure themselves and those around them by how much money they can earn. You must learn to flip this on its head and simply make it the consequence of what you choose to do and who you decide to be.

Now, I'm not here to say that every success and your wildest dreams will fall in your lap just because you leave your job, believe in your dreams, and you work hard. There are practicalities. If I honestly believe I will be the President of the United States in 2024, however hard I work, it is highly unlikely to come true. That's just due to the practical real-world realities of not living in the USA and not being an American citizen (and having little interest in politics.). I'm not talking about believing in mumbo jumbo here. I can't suddenly decide I'm Superman and really jump off the car park roof to fly off in to the sunset. I can't enter a TV talent show to sing because, well I can't sing that well. I ***can*** however be in control of realistic dreams and realities that I want to enter my life. And yes…***some*** of those can be wild and imaginative and can come true. Don't be scared to dream of reaching the stars, just don't go crazy and shoot for the heavens on your first attempt.

Now, not only have I crushed your dreams of learning the big secret for how to quit work well, and told you that you are wasting your time fantasising that others' lives are better than yours……it's time to kick you while you are down with another whopping great reality check.

Fact 3 - *Nobody* is out to get you or mess up your life

As well as my own 'I'm special' complex, I also felt hard done by because I suffered from some substantial health issues throughout my life. I, most likely as you do, had always felt that I was 'done to' by the world and the people around me. I always saw my situation as an inward projection that was placed on me by the world around me and was therefore, for the most part, well beyond my control. I believed I had little say and was subject to blind (bad) luck, bad health and other's opinions and actions. I always looked at the negative things in my life and saw them as unlucky, or unfair. Someone, somewhere, had a voodoo doll of me and was laughing their heads off sticking pins in my eyes (turned out to be my kidneys and my pancreas actually). It makes for a very bitter view on the world, but more importantly it is paralyzingly strong at stopping you from taking action to change your situation. It can make you feel very much like you have no control over your life. I would often not bother doing something positive, having played out the full scenario a dozen times inside my mind, coming up with more interesting and obscure ways as to how it wouldn't go my way. It's extremely easy and it can feel very safe to try and protect oneself from disappointment. This was ultimately the root cause of the problem for me. If I blamed all my feelings, situations, results, and life in general on the world around me, well…then I wouldn't ever be disappointed with anyone or anything, as I would always be right. The best example I have from my own experience was my last promotion at work. I was steadily moving along in a middle management role in a project management environment and after five years of hard schmoozing and grafting, I was desperate to get a Head of Service position. During a restructure several of these positions came up and I decided to talk to the Director of Service, and ask them for their advice on applying for the position. I arranged to meet them after work and wound myself up to be sure I was keen and concise and showed enthusiasm for the roles as, of course, life would be *so* much better once I had *this* job. It was late in the day and I stood in a foyer waiting for the Director to come through. There was not a single soul left on that floor of the building, so it was deathly quiet. Eventually they trotted into the room, smiled, and walked over to prop up next to me. Just me and them…..I was clear, friendly, but direct and to the point. After selling myself for ten minutes and receiving lots of exciting nods from the directo,r I finished by directly asking them. 'So..P (let's keep them anonymous), what do you think, could it be a good experience for me to apply for one of the Head of Service roles?'. 'Hmmm' they said looking around the room a little as they contemplated my question. 'To be honest Matt, not really, no'. That was it. No explanation, no softened blow, no lies even to just let me think I had a chance going through the process. Just those few words followed by a dead pan face looking straight in my eyes, waiting for a response. I was *so* emotionally invested in what I thought was the right thing at that point, that they may have just as well punched me in the face. It was a critical blow to my chest. Who the hell was this person? In fact, do they not realise how much I secretly think they themselves are a complete incompetent narcissistic fool? Do they not know how desperate I am for the institution to verify the emotional emptiness and heartache I experience everyday just falling into line like a good middle manager!!!!? Clearly, they didn't. So, ultimately like a good little boy I sucked it up, went back to work the next day and never applied for the promotion.

The reality was, as I look back now, is they just simply didn't see it the way I did. They weren't going out of their way to hurt me or trying to get me to throw myself out the window. They were just being honest and likely never thought about it again. I on the other hand, hated them for it, went out of my way to muddy their name, criticise them whenever I could and despised them from afar. And for what? Because I failed to understand that the world does not do unto us, but we do unto it! Even if they *had* wanted to be unreasonable and didn't particularly like me, then so what? Who were they to me, looking back years later. Nobody. I should have let the experience have zero impact on me, and done exactly what I wanted to do anyway. So, what could I have done? Two options. Never asked in the first place, applied, tried my best and realised that that was all I could do in any situation. Number two, asked them, listened, thanked them, applied, tried my best and realised that that was all I could do in any situation……. (Incidentally I got the same job a year later anyway, working for someone else…….I ended up hating it).

The fact of the matter is, that still years later I think the director probably remains a poor manager, because I would never talk to someone like that in a similar situation. However, what it taught me, was simply that these 'things' that happen in our lives, our interactions, our experiences…they are *all* within our control to some degree. Not how things happen and how people behave, but how we respond and how we chose to *act* because of them. I should have simply done what I wanted to do regardless of what they said.

I'm sure you can resonate in some way or another a similar situation in your working life like this where you have been hugely emotionally affected by it. And yes, it's easy for me to say,' oh just turn the other cheek, or forget about it'. After all I didn't do that. Yet, I realise now that you absolutely can if you allow yourself to choose to. At the time I was heavily sunk into a poor work life relationship and *everything* around me would gain an emotional response. It's not the individual situation that causes this, it is the longer-term situation we have put ourselves in, desperately trying to validate ourselves in a scenario that we simply don't belong. So if you do find yourself often having similar experiences at work, you need to think to yourself is this actually because I am not listening to myself? Is it perhaps that I am doing the wrong thing with my life?

I want you to try a simple exercise for me at this point. Don't worry you don't have to close your eyes, or find a quiet place. Simply think of the last two weeks and all the things that have happened that have either upset you, annoyed you, or given you any kind of unpleasant emotional response. Picture them all whizzing around in your head. Now pick one, the one that most sticks out for you. Imagine it like a TV or a picture floating and spinning round slowly in a circle above your head. Now how does it affect you? The likelihood is that it is *oppressing* you. It is pushing down on you, it is looking at you, it is shouting at you, or it is weighing you down. You quite probably feel one of these emotions or a very similar sense of depression. This Is because you are allowing the situation to 'do unto you' rather than you 'do unto it'. Now I'm not going to follow this up with a meditation lesson on how we make it go away or tell you to imagine you are floating out of your body. No, I simply want you to understand the principle that maybe at this stage of your life you are a person who allows those feelings to affect *how* you interact with the world. You are, as I was, someone who allows themselves to be 'done to'. I bet if you were to take yourself out of that situation and place a friend or loved one in your place, you could imagine yourself giving them completely different and appropriate advice on the situation, yes? I know I would. We are always ready to support friends and family in doing the right thing for them, but often neglect treating ourselves the same way. Right now, thinking back on Director P, if it had been my wife for instance in that situation, I would just simply have said to her 'stuff them'. 'they don't know you, if you want to go for it, do it'...." incidentally, given your reaction do you really want this job and to work there!?". It's a very small, but powerful change of perspective to begin treating yourself internally as you would treat your friends and loved ones.

Now, exposing some more truths and holding up some mirrors to you, I will help you change your point of view as we go through the following pages, slowly adjusting your view on yourself, the world, your expectations, and your realities.

Chapter 2 – Behaving like a hamster

Yes, a strange title for a chapter, but I think it's a worthy analogy and yes…. I am going to suggest to you that you are behaving like a hamster. Yes, a hamster. In fact, a very unhappy and sweaty hamster in an ever-accelerating hamster wheel. It's actually a very simple and powerful concept which should shine light on your situation and why you feel like you do.

Input. Reward. Consume. Repeat.

Those four words are the simplest explanation I can use to describe what most people like you and I are doing when going through working life in an unsatisfying career, and furthermore, why it is a broken process for us. It was definitely what I was doing for the best part of twenty years through my own career and something that is *very* difficult to see off your own back while in it. I have been lucky to make it through and have had a number of years to look back on the situation and diagnose it to within an inch of its life, which is why I have worked hard to simplify it as much as possible in order to help you. First, it's important to say that some people are lucky in a sense in that they just accept it as the way it is and crack on without a care in the world. Many others also find it a satisfying and comforting place to be. These are the people that turn up to their job, do what they can, go home and sleep like a baby. Unfortunately, I didn't feel like this and fought internally against it for all those twenty years, thinking that it was simply just how things were and what I must *make* myself do in order to get by in the world. This will likely be much the same as you feel. The bottom line is that this simple but powerful cycle for you and I just *does not work*. It doesn't mean there is anything wrong with us, it just means like I have said before, that we are just not in the right situation for us to be happy. It's destructive, it's close to madness, and it simply makes us feel trapped and miserable. The premise of this simple hamster cycle is that you are forced to produce something, an *output*….be it in a role making a physical artefact, or providing a 'time based' service to someone. Something, anything (many things!) that you don't particularly enjoy/absolutely hate/find soul sucking. This output that you then produce becomes the *input* to the owner (boss/company etc) of the hamster wheel. Simple, yes? Problem is…just as you think you are about to go mad and scream the building down, you are *rewarded* for this input.

Monthly, weekly, whenever. You end up getting ***paid***. You get given money by someone or some entity for this work; this output you have created that feeds the cycle. They buy your compliance! This then gives you some kind of small and short-lived gratification or feeling that it is worth all the hassle. Dealing with the idiots, falling asleep in a meeting, crawling through the hour and a half discussion whether your presentation should be with a red background or a blue one. It messes things up because it gives you a reason to carry on. Suddenly, you have been given something to make that output have some value to you. Why is it valuable? Because what you can do with that money is use it to reward yourself by using it to ***consume***. Consume a nice house (mortgage), consume some TV, consume a nice shiny new lease car, consume a meal out, consume your yearly holiday. Then at least you get the feeling that it was worth it. Finally you are being rewarded for the pain and boredom of the role you have, or the input you produce. You will at least have some kind of validation of why you do what you do, because after all if you find it boring, or worse even hate it, what idiot would do that for no reason right? Trouble is…the money runs low and you need more because you can't reward yourself without it. Luckily for you though the place where you work needs more of your outputs to input into its cycle. More reports, more artefacts, more toothpicks, washing machines, glossy brochures, or whatever. They need it because they need to feed the cycles of all the other employees, directors and shareholders and give them their rewards. So, once again you get paid some more. Eventually though you begin to feel that that amount of money isn't really hitting the spot any more. The car is a bit older, the house is too small for the family and you aspire for more consumption. What about that new job that will surely be better than this one? So, the natural thing to do is to work harder! You start to run harder and put *more* effort into the hamster wheel. You devote more of yourself to your role, work more hours, scrabbling for overtime, or for that pedestal of promotion. You become desperate for your yearly 'above average' personnel report from your line manager, so you can wallow in the satisfaction of gaining 1% more than the average yearly 2% pay increase. It's a process that has been designed over many, many years to do *exactly* what it does. To trap individuals in a cycle that appears to have no exit.

What I have just described, my friend, is your perpetual hamster wheel. The more you give of yourself, the more reward you crave to numb the emotional cost, the long hours, the awful boss, the fight for promotion. All these things make you run faster in the hamster wheel trying to gain *more* reward for *more* outputs so you can reward yourself with ***more*** consumption. That new TV, that new car, the expensive cordless vacuum. 'It will be alright when I have car X' or 'It'll be ok when I have £x in the bank'…right? What about that Holy Grail of yearly two-week holidays, far away from your everyday life? Oh, yes that's always top of the list. Why? Because you are so desperate to get as far away from your working life as you can, for just a short amount of time, giving you the opportunity to step out of that hamster wheel for just a moment. The other classic is 'well at least I'll be able to retire early on a nice pension and live out my dreams then'. Really? Says who? You have no idea what is going to happen to you tomorrow, let alone in retirement. And besides, who made the rule that says you have to ***earn*** a good retirement anyway? Where is it written that you have to work hard for forty years in a string of jobs you don't like just so you '***may***' enjoy a happy retirement? Sounds to me distinctly like serving life in prison, hoping one day for parole! Yet we are blinded and see it as just the way things are and not something we can change. Equally I for one very much enjoy what I am doing now and have a much different view on 'retirement' than I used to when I was in traditional employment. I actually don't see it as a fixed goal or something to aim for. I am very happy doing what I do and don't ever see a point where I want to stop. I actually spend way more of my time now doing things I want to, when I want to. When you are master of your own destiny, yes you have to work very hard, but your life is so much more within your own control. As a prime example, yesterday at 2pm I went to watch my son swim in a school competition. This doesn't sound much, but I organised my day around it and I left my house and went and watched him for a little over two hours. While I was there I had not one care other than watching him. A few other parents were there (most couldn't make it as they had 'work commitments'). Yet even of the ones that were there, several of them kept going outside answering their phone, typing emails and generally looking extremely stressed like they had been naughty and dared to duck out of work for a couple of hours. Knowing some of these very people well I can also guarantee you, these same people will likely do 4 to 6 hours extra work to 'make up' as a penance for daring to watch their child swim. Doesn't this truly sound like madness to you? It is! It simply isn't right to be in this type of situation. This is why I am now so grateful for how I live my life now. I go back to the idea that being rewarded one day by 'retirement' means nothing to me anymore. Sure, as I get older, I am highly likely to slow down or do less, but as what I do now is not a chore, I don't see it as something that I wish to stop. I feel for sure now that for the rest of my life I may well choose to do 'something' to keep me occupied well into my 70's….if fate allows. So like those parents at the swimming competition (or worse those that couldn't even make it!), being in a position where you feel trapped by what you are doing, puts you in such a negative and difficult place. You are serving this ridiculous prison sentence in the hopes that when you are old you *may* be set free! I keep saying it, but I will reiterate... there is nothing wrong with it not being right for you. Surely you can see that this might not be such a great idea for you? You don't just have to put up with things in order to 'make it'. You deserve to do more than just make it through your life if the best you can look forward to is retirement after years of sacrifice. You do *not* have to conform, you do *not* have to do what everyone else does. You also do *not* have to be scared that if you don't follow the socially acceptable ways, you will somehow 'miss out' or be 'left behind'. It simply isn't true. Once again I am confident that if you saw a friend of yours in the same position, miserable and trapped in their job, you would encourage them to make a change and wish for them to look for happiness? Many people in my life have said how much happier and healthier I seem and how happy they are for me. Yet these same people won't look at themselves and wish the same? We are again in the same position as where YOU would want a friend to make the change, but don't care for yourself enough to do the same? This needs to change and it needs to change now.

I told you in my introduction that I just upped and left my job five years ago, right before I ***promised*** you that I was not any different from you yes? I'm not a liar, I would be a pretty sick individual to write a book about helping people live an alternative life, for it to be a joke right?! It's a cliché but there is the classic saying that we have but one life. Do you really think it is ok to sacrifice your own to something that makes you stressed and miserable, just because you are scared to make a change? Your family will still love you! Your friends (the true ones) will still care about you and support you! You can do this…

So now I have had my little rant to try and get your juices going, I have a few simple questions to ask you about your own little hamster wheel. Hopefully this will help you realise exactly what you are doing running your little legs off, and prove to that right now you need to make a change….

Here it is…When you last came back from holiday of more than a week away, did you have a feeling of loss, anxiety, depression, or hopelessness when you realised you were returning to work tomorrow? Do you get to the point at work where things are so bad, that you ***have*** to book something to look forward to? Maybe a holiday, weekend away, trip to see family. Anything, just so you can cope with a few more weeks in your job?

Well, if the answer is yes to both these questions…. reward yourself with a hamster treat! It took me a long time to allow myself to accept I was in this situation. Realising it is easy. I will bet you already subconsciously know it, or I may have just triggered that last jigsaw piece that made it all clear. This is not the problem. The problem is accepting it and ***doing something about it***. Why is this the problem? Because you have invested so much time, effort, blood, and tears running in your hamster wheel. You will likely firmly believe that if you step out of it you will have wasted all those years of building up the speed and suddenly find yourself going absolutely nowhere! You will highly likely feel it is 'too late' for you to jump out the wheel. After I realised that I was on the wheel, for years I had been convinced that as soon as I stepped away and left my 'career', it would be over. All of the hard work, the growing stress, anger, and in my case hatred, of what I had had to do, would have been for nothing. The feeling of having run a thousand miles to be told it was in the wrong direction is a very scary concept. This is a huge aspect of why so many carry on doing it. The enormity of the potential ***loss*** is overwhelming and paralysing to most. It appears in front of you like a massive void. It is an incredibly scary concept to feel you may have wasted your life, and just simply can't stop running for fear of regret. This feeling is perfectly normal, but it simply isn't true. I want you to imagine this second that you have just lost your job and been told for whatever reason you will never be able to get another job again. Think hard about what that feels like. Awful? Yes. Terrible, frightening, all consuming. What on Earth will I do to live? How will I pay my bills? What will people think of me? It's particularly important for me and you at this point to acknowledge the enormity of how this makes you feel. I want you to feel anxious, to feel frightened thinking of if this were to ever happen. For me I simply couldn't see a way past it. Yet, as you know I have made this very dark and scary leap and can tell you what it is really like. And the answer may surprise you.

It's amazingly simple. It's like sitting on the edge of the plane at 10,000 feet, absolutely bricking it and then finally taking all your courage to jump out. Five minutes later you are on the ground having free fallen, opened the 'chute' and landed safely back to normality. Five minutes ago, it was the most monstrously scary thing you have ever done…and now, well it was great! This situation you are in is *exactly* the same. Yes, there is a moment of tremendous anxiety, worry and the great unknown. But ultimately it is just a moment and on the other side lies the truth you are looking for. All it takes is the courage to know that behind that thin veil of great fear is another world. Another place. One I very much like hanging out in and would love to see you in. The true value I can add here, is to prove that it is a simple moment in time, that I have achieved, and proved it is survivable. All you have to do it is just push it and its gone. I remember my own experience very well the day I left my job. It was almost an instantaneous switch. The fear, the anxiety, the loss. It all started to vanish as I took each step towards the exit door. I suddenly realised as I looked at everyone around me that I had just discovered the barriers were fake. It was just the thin sheet of paper with all my fears and anxieties on it, yet one tiny push and it collapsed like a deck of cards. Everything suddenly became so clear to me in an instant. Of course, I was nervous, I was unsure of what was to come, yet I still felt such a huge weight lifting off me. Now sadly (although I genuinely wish I could), I can't jump out of your plane for you. It is something you are going to need to do for yourself. However, I hope I am starting to make you realise that you *can* do it, because I am right down on the ground waiting for you.

Thinking seriously about the thought I posed a few moments ago, that you could *never* get another job; do you honestly deep down believe that your life would be over and you could provide nothing or do nothing? Do you not think that you have the skills and capability to do ***something***? You have capabilities, you have core skills, you have passion! You have not wasted your time doing what you have been doing. It has got you to here and you can use it as an experience to now take you further. You just need to give yourself the opportunity to flourish in the right environment.

So, what we can do together, here and now is ***plan*** for it to take place, execute it and then it is done! Much like a real skydive, you are not going to just jump in the nearest plane, fly up to 10,000 feet and throw yourself out. It could be messy. You would train for it. You would look at sky diving schools, their online reviews, videos, get instruction, learn safety measures ….. all these things before you get ready to jump out of a plane. The same is necessary here to make the move and to quit work well. I'm not talking about being reckless here! We will explore the practicalities of getting prepared for this in Section Two.

Right now, however, we are going to look more into the various aspects, 'the hurdles', of your fears and anxieties that cause inaction for the actual jump itself, and look to give you the emotional strength to attack the barriers in your own way, to then find the courage to do it.

Chapter 3 – The hurdles

One thing I am without doubt a self-made expert on is excessive emotional thought. Anxiety, overthinking and unhealthy emotional investment in all aspects of my life has always been at the forefront of my mind. I know all there is to know about being anxious in everyday life, of what the future holds and of being scared of failure. I was, and still am to an extent, a grand-master, at hiding it behind a confident outward persona. For years, this persona interacted with the world on my behalf, while I furiously scrabbled my way through my working career. These days, however, I am much more centred and happier with myself and also frankly much more open about my feelings and emotions. I do strive to continue working hard on being much less anxious in all aspects of my life. I can assure you I have been there and done it when it comes to mental and emotional health. So, we can discuss together getting yourself in a much better place mentally and emotionally too.

In this chapter we are going to explore the key emotional and sociological blockers that I believe you need to understand, and to *begin* to overcome, in order to give yourself the greatest chance of success in making the jump. I have used my own experiences, and those of the many people I have talked with since making the jump, to formulate the base set of 'blockers'. These blockers in one form or another, cause the vast majority of the stumbling blocks that have already stopped you from making the changes you so desperately want. We will discuss them individually in turn.

1. The Fear Factor

The first thing to conquer is the same type of fear you experience when doing that parachute jump I talked about for the first time. Imaging yourself sitting there on the edge of the plane, paralysed.... with *fear*. It is not a normal biological situation to sit 10,000 feet in the air and decide to jump out of the only thing that is keeping you alive. Despite having grown hugely as a human being since quitting work both emotionally and mentally, I am very assured physically jumping out of an actual plane would be a *very* tough experience for me to overcome. Yet it is very similar to how our own internal reality treats the world of work. This is because we are programmed to believe that jumping from our job is not the 'normal' or right thing to do and that it is fraught with danger. So how do so many people make the jump for an actual sky dive anyway? Ultimately, very few people get in the plane and come back down with their tail between their legs having not jumped. You are much more likely to know someone who has completed a skydive, than to know someone who came back in the plane. Yet in some ways it doesn't make sense. Given the huge stress, fear and anxiety the majority of people feel in the plane, why are there not more people out there who never jumped? The answer in its simplest form is that the jumpers don't stop feeling the fear, they just happen to jump anyway! The reason most people are able to jump out of a plane is that despite the hundreds of fears and anxieties traveling around their head, it is an alien situation and they don't have years and years of pre-programmed experience in that situation. What do you think would happen if you took someone up into a plane, dangled them out the door while telling them it was really dangerous for them to jump. What if you repeated this daily for decades, then suddenly one day, gave them a parachute while they were up there? Do you think they would jump out? No, of course not! However, the circumstance on that day is the same as the first. There is only one simple action they need to take to make it go away. And that is take a single step out of the plane. The problem is the years on conditioning against it. There is a fundamental change we need to make for you, in that we need to *simplify* your fears, package them, and practically deal with them. This way you then have a number of simple clear steps to perform, rather than focusing on the complex historical issues and the abyss of the 'drop' from your job in its entirety. We will talk more about packaging and planning the jump later on, but for now we will discuss a little more about the fear itself.

The bottom line is you are scared on a number of levels when thinking about living your life differently. What will happen to me? Will it be a mistake? Will I ruin my career? Will I be poor? Will I lose my house/my partner/my car? You may also feel you will have no idea what will happen to you if you do it.......well the bottom line is you are correct! You *don't* know what will happen, because nobody knows what will happen in the future. It's impossible to know. Not just in this situation though, but in *every* situation of your life. Will you get run over tomorrow? Nobody knows. Will you win the Lottery next week? Will you get promoted this year? Will you be made redundant soon? Nobody knows. Yet, you will still go out and go to work tomorrow. You may still buy your lottery ticket this week. Fundamentally, there is no difference to these situations and the situation of quitting work.

A little interesting fact for you:
'According to the United States Parachuting Association, there are an estimated 3 million parachute jumps per year, and the fatality count is only 21 (for 2010). That's a 0.0007% chance of dying from a skydive, compared to a 0.0167% chance of dying in a car accident (based on driving 10,000 miles annually). In layman's terms, you are about 24 times more likely to die in a car accident than in a skydiving one.'

So, you are literally 24 times more likely to die driving about this year, than jumping out of a plane (with a parachute of course)! This doesn't however physically change how the later is more scary it in any way other than our own perception of the situation. This again is because of the conditioning. Most of us have driven or been driven in a car thousands of times, so we are pre-conditioned to it. Much like we you and I are preconditioned to work a job for a living. So, if you can get your head round this principle, you can empower yourself to make this apparently very difficult and scary decision of leaving your current work life. Seriously! Yes, it's a large and complex situation to quit your career, but fundamentally it is no different from any other decision you make a hundred times each day!

Another reason you are fearful of it, as was I, is that your job/career has been built up into something it isn't, over a long period of time. It has become an all-encompassing, life changing, immovable object that has stood in your way potentially for years and years. I knew things weren't right from about 25 years old. Nearly 20 years! Imagine the poor person sitting on the edge of the plane getting ready to jump for 20 years! You'd die of fear! Twenty long years of having this shadow hang over me, scaring the life out of me anytime I thought about it. Imagining it was the impenetrable barrier, that impossible fight. Yet on the day I actually quit work and walked out the door, as I told you earlier, it practically disappeared in an instant. Sure, I was anxious, worried about what I was going to do, but I had just jumped out the plane and the world around me was exactly the same. I was still me, I hadn't instantly died, I hadn't turned into a three headed monster. I was *exactly* the same person inside that I was before. The beauty was though that instantly I felt as if I had revealed myself to the world (not in a creepy way,) and a huge weight had been lifted off me. I didn't have to pretend any more. I didn't have to get on with people I didn't like or didn't respect. I didn't have to be somewhere specific each day at a certain time. I didn't have to ask someone else's permission if I wanted to spend the day with my family. I didn't have to wear clothes I didn't want to, so I looked a certain way. In that first instant it's unbelievably liberating. Looking behind you, you realise that the huge immovable fear never really existed at all except in your mind. The decision you have just made is just like any other. You will almost instantly have a feeling that it was never there. That lifelong weight, that shadowed your whole being is simply a thin fake veil of unnecessary fear and fabricated emotions. You will feel the same rush as the person who jumps out the aeroplane for their parachute jump. It is just like that split second of jumping into the unknown, which is followed (for most of them!) by the exhilaration of the jump, the huge feeling of accomplishment that they have done that.

Now you ***will*** need courage to make that jump, just as anyone does, as much as you will need to keep this courage to change the way you do things. What I needed to gain the strength to do it, and what I will help you to do, is to come at it from two directions. The first is having a ***plan***. We will talk about this more as we progress into Section Two, but again, like our parachute jump, we aren't just going to go to the first person that advertises it, miss the induction training and just hop on the plane hoping for the best. No…we are going to research, plan, and train for the jump. We are going to maximise our chances of a ***safe jump***. We will make it as safe as possible. However, we will ***also*** accept that even though we plan, we have to realise that some aspects of it will be out of our control, and some aspects of it will require a leap of faith to achieve. In many ways, the planning is the easy part, even though it will take you much longer than the split second of actually making the jump.

Another reason you are as fearful as the jumpers are, is that we naturally fear situations that we cannot understand or control. However, many people have learnt to accept the effects of change and uncertainty, and to accept that there are situations they will be in that are unknown. Again, looking at my own path, I was very much taken up in envisioning my lifelong journey through my working career. Planning out promotions, salaries, training milestones over the coming years. 'By 2025 you may be Head of Service'…'by 2030 you may want to be a director'. It is a very comforting situation that both helps to stave off fear of the future and also supports the mechanism of the hamster wheel. It gives you purpose for this crazy working life. You will highly likely be the same. You may have 'great plans' for where your career is going, what you are going to get paid, what job you will have in 10 years' time. Alternatively, you may have reached mid-life and think 'well I've got this far, I'll just sit here comfortably and wait for retirement'. Trouble is you aren't accounting for the unknown, for the uncertainty. What happens if you get ill? What happens if your company folds? What happens if you get run over? What happens if World War 3 turns up?! I have worked through this and come out the other side. I am much more comfortable with the idea of not being able to truly know what I am doing from month to month or even day to day now. My reality hasn't changed, I'm not suddenly living in a different world. It's just my appreciation and my perception of the world around me. The only thing that has actually changed is my approach. I plan my work; I have new ideas, I experience lots of change, but I also allow myself to go with the flow substantially more than I did before. Many people who knew me before have commented on my bravery or my confidence and how it has changed since I have taken my own path in life. This sometimes makes me smile as the reality is it hasn't. I still have fears, I still have doubts, but what I have done is learnt to build my courage and accept them as part of any and all of life's journeys. It is not a confidence problem to overcome this barrier. You don't have to have no fear, you just need more courage to accept it is OK to feel it.

For me another realisation that helped me greatly, was that I am utterly and completely responsible for everything that happens in my life. This is 100% true for you too. As we touched on earlier, like me, you may have spent part of your life blaming others, or the environment around you, for what has happened to you. The painful truth (which ironically, I think deep down you already know but haven't accepted yet) is that you are wrong. I was wrong. I was so very, very wrong that I could barely look at myself in the mirror. We have already discussed that nobody owes you anything. Nobody has ruined your life. Nobody has made your life decisions. Nobody stops you from going to the gym. Nobody stopped you from applying for that promotion. Nobody decided what salary you are worth. ***Every*** aspect of your life has been created and manipulated by your own reality of what is in front of you. Everything you do, think, or say has a direct impact on every aspect of your life. 'You are wrong' I hear you say. 'What about that promotion I didn't get? How is that my fault?'. Well, I'll tell you how. Did you ***really*** want that promotion? I mean did you ***really*** 'life and death' want that promotion? You didn't because you didn't get it. How many times did you apply for it, or a similar role in your own company? …. How many times did you look outside your current company and apply for a role of similar level with other companies?.... How many evenings did you spend writing your application and practicing interview techniques with your partner or work colleagues?....... How many hours did you spend on the internet researching the role, interview techniques, industry news?......How many people in the new part of the business did you take for a coffee to find out about what they do?..... How many times did you meet with the manager of the new role to find out what they were looking for? I could finish the book with a thousand more of these questions, but I think you get the point. The answer is even if you did do all of the above, you didn't do them enough! And the reason you didn't do them or do them enough is that you didn't take personal responsibility for the outcome. 'Oh, I'll just apply for the role and see what happens'. Well guess what, you didn't get the job. This is what needs to change in your head. It was yours to get, it was yours to lose. Maybe the journey would have been extremely long and difficult, maybe you needed to do two more years in role working your backside off, or training to get qualifications, but it was still within your grasp if you *truly* wanted it with every breath. This is exactly the same as now, making that leap, changing your life. For many of the people I talk to, it's almost as if they are waiting for permission from someone to make such a huge change. Who?! Your partner? God? The man next door? *You* need to give *you* the permission. The trouble is that you haven't for the last twenty years (or however long), so it's a hard thing to do. But that's all there is to it. I can talk till I'm blue in the face telling you that nobody is waiting around the corner to give this permission to you, you ultimately have to just 'man/woman/person up' and take it on yourself. I can guide you through this of course, but you are responsible for that first step out of the plane. You must realise that you are in control, it is not out of control. Feel the fear, accept it, it will never go. Only then can we look at the other aspects of your reality that are stopping you. *If* you can conquer them all and truly realise that you are in control then that first step will be so much easier, and you will have the courage to do it. I can on the other hand though give you a little nudge in the right direction by telling you another story and a well-known fact that you can look up………

Roger Bannister broke the four-minute mile (running) in 1954. *Nobody* had ever done it and for years and years 'experts' had said it was impossible. Forty-six days later a man called John Landy did it. Within a year of him breaking the record ***three other runners did it in the same race together***. Roger

Bannister had given the psychological *approval* for others to believe it was achievable, that it was doable, that it was 'OK' to run a four-minute mile. Now if John Landy had had the right mindset in the previous few weeks, he could have given himself that approval and been the first to do it. Surely nobody thinks that an extra couple of weeks training that John did was coincidently the extra final weeks strength or fitness he needed to break the four minutes? It just 'happened' that the first two people to break four minutes *ever*, managed to do it within 46 days of each other? Of course not. John had a psychological barrier believing it was impossible, that was broken by knowing someone else had done it, therefore subconsciously telling himself he could do it too. Well, I'm sitting here five years after I quit my highly paid management career talking to you directly, saying that I have done it and I give you permission to let yourself do this! I promise you from the bottom of my heart once again that I am no different from you. I am a normal everyday guy who has done something many see as extraordinary. I didn't discover any secrets, I didn't have a guru guide me, I didn't follow an expensive self-help online course. I worked with myself, my mind, my reality, and I just did it. I am openly sharing with you everything I felt, did, and changed to get here, with the promise that if you so decide, you too can give yourself permission now too. I have *proved* from my own jump that there is no barrier, it isn't impossible and you can do it. Remember the fear will be there, it won't go away, but you can accept it and achieve this change regardless.

2. Everyone else can't be wrong…right?

Hundreds of millions of people all over the world get up 5 days a week (some more, some less) and 'work' in a typical 9-5 job. It's a simple fact. For generations, it's just been how it is. The vast majority of people in the western world finish school, college or university and get themselves employed in various jobs, earning a wage, until they reach some type of retirement age, while taking two weeks holidays each summer and engaging in social activities at the weekend. This is the hamster behaviour we have talked about, where our society is built around the cycle of output and reward. Everything fits nicely into little compartmentalised boxes, keeping the masses in order trundling around the wheel. Much of the reason for this is that capitalism has placed a divide between working and leisure and turned work into a commodity. People have 'worked' since the beginning of the stone-age. Hunting, farming, building etc, it's not a new thing. Yet as humankind evolved and industrialisation and capitalism began to flourish, work was pigeon-holed into this commodity. Something measurable, be it an hourly rate, a production output, a salary.

But, regardless of how it was done and is done now, it remains, at least for now a tangible 'thing'. This is ultimately what has created the entity of a 'job', which in turn has fabricated the entity of a 'career'. This commodity is how the majority of the population follow the same trend and have jobs/careers that pay them a wage to sustain their existence. So…surely you and I must be wrong thinking this is not the right thing to do? Why are these millions of people working Monday to Friday to be paid a fixed sum at the end of the week/month, if it's not a good idea? Perhaps you should just knuckle down and play it safe? Yes, perhaps you should. You know what….. let's forget about the whole thing. Close the book, send it back and ask for a refund..*or* perhaps you could join me in thinking to yourself that 'everybody' is not always right. It's not that long ago that the general consensus would be that the car (automobile) was a noisy, smelly, pointless and expensive waste of time and money. The majority of the world's population either had no idea what one was or couldn't believe you would want to swap out your trusty horse and cart to have one. You could go back as close in time as your great-grandfather to find that opinion. A mere couple of generations. Now some would argue that it was so new for its time, it's not fair to suggest general opinion was wrong about the car, because nobody knew its potential or could determine the changes it might bring. Well…hello?!

Can't we say the same about working differently? Perhaps it's just one of those ideas that has not gained general support yet, nor does 'everyone' know the beauty and benefits that it can bring to people's lives. The reality here is that 'general opinion' is changeable, and in fact it can be very quickly changed. So whether you perceive it as 'right' or 'wrong', it is only momentary anyway. Even in our own lifetime (if you are a similar age to me) you could reference something like the Internet. In its infancy I would suggest that most people were either indifferent or thought the idea was even laughable. Sending an electronic letter to your granny instead of writing to her and posting it! How quaint. But look at was has happened since its inception in 1973. I remember clearly when I was about 14 in the early 1990's, that my older brother and a friend came up with the idea of listing houses for sale on the internet. The idea would be to have a little paragraph about the property and then a series of photographs showing the internal rooms. Clear as day I remember practically rolling around the floor laughing. 'Who the hell is going to spend hundreds of thousands of pounds on a house by looking at pictures of it on the internet?'....oh boy what a really strange idea that was right?!……….. (sadly for him it never happened, like many great ideas, so he doesn't own Rightmove unfortunately!). That's just one small example of my own thoughGbut imagine asking the majority of society their opinion on the power of the internet now, particularly anyone under 21. My God, my niece would probably drop dead if she found she lost her internet connection for a day and couldn't use social media to convince the world her life is wonderful. Therefore there is no reason to think that the same can't now be said for what is described as a 'job'. Yes capitalism is here to stay very likely for the long term, but so much has changed since our parents and grandparents used to work a job. The flexibility of the internet, mobile phones, learning technologies, artificial intelligence, access to on demand production facilities, access to training, globalisation.... I could go on for a whole page on the tools and changes that are right there in front of you to help you make significant changes in the way you work. This means there is no better time than ***right now*** to do things differently. The world changes, always has and always will. We must try and remember that the pivotal thing to remember about 'everyone' and 'popular opinion' is that it is a snapshot in time. It is not long living, it is not black and white, and it is neither absolutely right nor absolutely wrong. It may well be in as little as 25-50 years that popular opinion laughs in the face of having a 9-5 office job. It may well be that by that point we are all flexible workers who ultimately work where, when and at what we want. Take the impact of COVID-19 as an example of major change. A natural disaster that was beyond anyone's control, but has for millions, fundamentally changed the structure of their working life. Working from home, hybrid working, Zoom meetings. Nobody could have predicted the system wide impact the virus has had. So our and our children's future 'career' may well be defined completely differently for any number of reasons. In a nutshell, what I'm trying to convey to you is that change is constant and often disruptive regardless of what you are doing. Opinion is forever changing and the world is in constant flux, so, don't assume there is any kind of real permanence in what you are currently doing anyway.

Now if that isn't enough to convince you, we can look at the simpler side of 'going against the grain' of popular opinion. Let's look through another little thought exercise. If you think hard enough, at some point in your life you have had an opinion that did not conform to the group of people around you. Even something as basic as a quiz night or trivia game with friends, or perhaps a lunch time political discussion at work. There are countless times in our lives where we find ourselves outnumbered two, five or even ten to one. Yet in some situations we can have such strong resolve, that we are willing to fight against those greater numbers often to the metaphorical death. So, think of one of those scenarios from past years and contemplate how you felt, how you strongly defended your belief/your opinion, despite the larger number against you. How did you feel? What did you do? I bet you felt strong. I bet you felt willing to fight. So now answer me the following question.

What *exact number* of opposing opinions or people would it have taken before you were no longer willing to fight for what felt right for you to? Let's say the point where you would have just bowed down and conformed to the mass opinion. There *will* be a number. As an example we could say the situation was during a pub quiz team and you wanted to answer 'A' instead of your whole team who wanted to answer 'B'. There may have been four or five people on your team who were all against you. Now, imagine that all of a sudden you became part of the biggest online quiz team ever created and there were a million people who wanted to answer B and you wanted to answer A. The question hasn't changed, neither has your resolve that you are right. However, I bet you would for sure feel doubt and pressure to change your mind and 'conform' to answer B anyway though yes? Of course, you would, that much pressure, two million eyes looking at you. The problem (and indeed the solution) in these circumstances is when we break it down and give a specific answer to the basic question. Exactly how many

would be needed to make that conforming behaviour come in to play?

Is it 2 people? Is it 14? Perhaps you are willing to go as high at 567, or even 1965. Maybe you're a badass and would stand firm at 23,565 team members in your very large pub quiz. The reality is you can't give me that ***exact figure***. A figure that you absolutely believe is the ceiling for your willingness to still have a different opinion to others, or to fight for a different belief, or take a different direction. The reason you can't give me a figure is because in reality there isn't one. It's all about perception and psychological pressure. If you can accept that the opinion of one other is different from yours, then you can accept it for ten. If you can accept ten people have a different opinion to you then you can accept it for a hundred. And so on, until you reach the majority of the population. It doesn't mean they are wrong, and you are right. It simply means it is not for you and you no longer feel the pressure to conform with a large group of people. Of course, it is more complex than the Pub quiz question, but the principle remains exactly the same. Physiologically, a large number is a scary thing. But it's also difficult to quantify, which then often means we will judge it with emotion rather than on an individual measured opinion.

Your ***opinion*** never changed at the quiz, but your doubts, fears and subconscious ***overcame*** your resolve that you were right.

Let me give you another example. Say I gave you a bag of rice. It has 100 grains in it. It would be pretty small. I ask you to count them and if you do, I'll give you a free two-week beach holiday to anywhere you want to go…all inclusive! You look at it, you assess it and you obviously say yes. It may take you a couple of minutes maybe. So now imaging each day I gave you that same bag with one more rice grain in it, day after day. 101, 102, 103, 104. No big deal I'm sure, and you would happily carry on each day counting rice and bagging the holiday day after day. Except ***eventually*** there would be a point in the future where you would look at the bag and just think to yourself 'I can't do it, it's too much, I won't have the patience, I can't manage that.' It is inevitable and would happen for everyone, but nobody knows exactly when. Everyone would have a different number for the day they give up. Some will be lazy and maybe get to a few thousand grains, but others may go much further in to the tens, or even hundreds of thousands. That is not the main point here though. What is the point is that ***everyone*** the day before they stopped would have completed the count successfully and just 1 grain of rice would tip them over the edge and change the outcome? This perception scenario is exactly the same one that stops us going against general opinion. It's the compounded growth and pressure that eventually, for no obvious reason to our conscious mind, changes our perception and emotional reaction to the situation. However, if we understand it is only 1 grain of rice more, or one more member on the quiz team, or one more friend who thinks you are mad quitting work…doesn't it make it more manageable? When we are able to break it down in to being ***just a number***, we can suddenly realise that there is no definitive switch point of any real value. There is no major change between the bags of rice with 48,780 and 47,781. It's the psychological blockers that we have that suddenly stops us in our tracks. When worrying about popular opinion on you making these changes, it is exactly the same mentality you need in order to overcome the fears and doubts that have until now caused your inaction. Just make sure if you feel yourself waning you think about your single extra grain of rice!

As well as the pressure of majority opinion, you will at some point on this journey also need to deal with the splinter groups. Individuals or small groups from whom will do their best to keep you in their collective and destroy your chances. Beware them! I did mention earlier in our conversation, that I would cover this a little more from my own experience with my pier group. On the whole when I first decided to make the jump, my family and friends were very supportive, as they had been for many other parts of my life. Yes, there were some that perhaps showed some concern and whether it was the right thing for me to do, but on the whole, it felt like it was coming from a place of caring, so I had no issue with it. However, at some point, like I was, you will be blindsided by a friend or family member who will not be so supportive. As soon as I told a particular friend of mine that I was looking to quit work and do my own thing, they instantly become very aggressive and defensive of my current situation. 'Why on earth would you want to do that?' ….'are you stupid?'…'you've got a great job?..'what are you going to do for money?'….'this is a really bad idea?'. I was very taken aback…. shocked. I tell you now this genuinely hurt me and shook my resolve. I was actually also very surprised at the time, as it was a friend that I wouldn't have expected to be like that. It was someone I had worked with closely for many years and we had developed a close relationship outside of work too. It knocked me back quite significantly. When it is someone close like this, be it family or friend, it can be a very difficult set of feelings to process. You are stretching your hand out for support, for some semblance of that permission we secretly so crave, from someone who you probably have a very high opinion of. Yet suddenly they turn around and kick you in the teeth and you have the doubt come flooding back. If your close friend or family member doesn't think it's a good idea then perhaps this isn't a great idea, right? Maybe they are right, and you should rethink this. Wrong. For many years I cared too much about others' opinions of what I was doing and what they thought of me. Was I seen as a 'success', was I doing a good job as a son, a father, a friend? And I can tell you now, it is time well and truly ***wasted***. Why? Because every one of those people (although without malice) is doing it for one of only two fundamental reasons. Fear, or jealousy. They either fear for you on some level on the basis of their own barriers to making such dramatic life changes, or they are jealous that you might just make it out there in the big scary world 'on your own' without them. Simple fact. There are no other reasons. What reasoning is there to be so against their friend or loved one trying to do something in their life that could make them immeasurably happier? There isn't. Please do not get dragged into this. Yet, also please don't blame them for it, as they are likely going through the same fears internally that you are trying to conquer. It is highly likely that my own friend who took such offence to the idea was, at some level, concerned for my wellbeing. They were likely overwhelmed with negative feelings from their own internal battles. It is more than likely that any one that does this to you ***does*** care for you dearly, but they are unable to process past the fear and/or jealousy to see that it may be what is best for you. You may just need to image them as the rare friend you took sky diving with you, that couldn't do it and then came down sheepishly inside the plane. Of course, they are not going to want to hear about your experience or how great it was/ is going to be. They are fearful and deflated that they couldn't do it and you could. You are doing something they are unable to do. Perhaps a good idea might be for you to lend them this book after you finish reading it.....

I can look back on my life now and identify dozens of situations and conversations where these exact blockers happened to me and stopped me from making my own powerful choices. I even recall several times where I was hurt and angry that someone I knew was moving on to something else in their life. If we are truthful, we have all actually been on the other side of these situations at some point. What I would say though now I am several years into my different way of life, is all these types of situations ever left me was regret. Regret for listening to my negativity and fears and a feeling of wishing I had made my own jump earlier.

Now, all of this is not to say that asking others and listening to feedback from those that are close to you is not a good idea. Sure, it is. Invite people to input on your thoughts, your plans, your ideas. Input and advice can be extremely empowering. Just make sure you understand the difference between constructive feedback and opinion. Opinion will be born of someone's inward facing views on their own 'done to' journey. It will not add value and will have negative impact on your changes. It is fine to hear it, to listen and politely disagree, or even just wait it out and then erase it from your mind. Constructive feedback will be genuine questioning and reasoning as to what you need to think about, or what situations you may find yourself in. It will *add* fuel to the fire of confronting the fear, or make for better planning in your strategy. Gain input. Ignore opinion. It is of course ok to care what others think, we would not be human if we were not affected by it. Yet it is *not* ok for you to make decisions based on it that are detrimental to your own health and wellbeing.

3. Timing

This is all great stuff, but maybe now is not the right time for me, you say. Ok, that's a fair comment. Maybe you don't have enough money saved up, or perhaps you haven't got your head round the idea fully. Maybe you want to give the chance of promotion just one more year, or wait and see what this year's pay rise is going to be. These things, on the face of it, are very decent and legitimate reasons to stay doing exactly what you are doing. The problem here though is that you probably have been doing that already for years. In reality, you will not feel different about the situation any more this year than last, unless you change your outlook. I never ever felt I was really truly ready to make the change until I *made* myself change my view on the situation. If we don't break the same mindset for you, you too will be unable to make the move and will only realise this when it's too late. You'll be looking back at your life, wishing you had done things differently. For nearly twenty years I would always find a reason why it was not a good time to make this kind of change. I didn't have enough money saved. I didn't have the right frame of mind. The economy was slow, I felt unwell, I didn't feel motivated enough at that particular moment, blah, blah, blah. I'm sure you can also come up with a long, long list of great reasons why tomorrow is not the right time. This is all totally normal and I don't want you to panic that we can't get over this. Remember, I have, and you can too. Again, I am no different from you. So, what I want you to do is make your thoughts tangible. Actually, start to create that long list of reasons stopping you and physically put them to paper. Get yourself a pen and notepad and take an hour one evening when you have some time alone to really dig deep into your mind and list every one of your very legitimate reasons as to why timing is important, and now is not the right time to make the jump from your job. Maybe my own ones above I listed are valid to you, or maybe you have others, but just jot down some really good solid reasons why tomorrow is not the right time to make a move on this change. Stop reading until you have done this exercise.

Now you've done that we can go through your list and straight off the bat, without knowing you, I can give you most of them right now off the top of my head:
1. You don't have enough money saved up as a safety net
2. You don't know what you want to do
3. You have too many emotional and/or financial responsibilities (mortgage, children, bills etc)
4. You don't have the skills/discipline/personal faith to make it on your own
5. You are scared you may fail and/or not be able to sustain your lifestyle and that of your family
6. You worry what others may think
7. You will be throwing your career away

Sure, you may have a few others, but now you have the list in front of you, take each one individually and (give or take) you should be able to tick most (or all) of them off against a version of the list I have created above. And this shouldn't really be a surprise to you either. The reason for this is because they are familiar to us all. All these are very good reasons that have been fabricated in our minds by running the hamster wheel. ***Everyone*** feels like this when looking to jump. The thing is though how many of them actually relate to timing? Very few. Look at your list and determine how many of these can be genuinely improved by having more time to deal with them. Unless you change your outlook considerably, the only ones that your time could potentially have effect on are related to money. Therefore, what chance have you got to feel the time is right if you are unable to affect most of these blockers with more time anyway? None. There is a reason you didn't quit work at 20, or 30, or 40 or whenever. The reality is that ***none*** of the reasons above are reasons not to want to improve your quality of life and find true happiness at whatever point in time you choose.

These are just various versions of your core fears and nothing truly related to timing. They are again more fabrications, smoke and mirrors that get in the way of us making the right life decisions. They are ever present blockers that you have constructed while enduring your journey in the hamster wheel. They are built in survival mechanisms you have created in your subconscious to validate to your conscious mind why you do what you do. I'm not saying you have 'made them up' but by me already knowing most of them without us meeting, surely it proves to you that it is just human nature that you have the same concerns as anyone else in the same position? It goes back to the similarities between us all. You are not that different. I had the same fears and reasons why I didn't quit…..yet I still managed to do it.

The bottom line is fear and the unknown brings negativity and an inability to make positive, proactive decisions. We naturally look for ways to disguise it as something else or to validate to ourselves why we don't make these changes. Fear will manifest itself in a whole number of strange ways that ultimately cause us to fail to make decisions. It is completely paralysing if not controlled or put into proportion.

So, let's take a look at the only one on the list that truly actually exists outside of our own mind. That is the question of not having enough money. Now, think very carefully on this one. Is there a specific monetary amount (that is achievable, so not £5 million), where you *honestly* believe it would make you comfortable enough psychologically, and it would be enough of a financial cushion, to allow you to quit your job tomorrow without any fear or doubt? I am confident that you don't truly have an achievable figure in mind right? Maybe you have a sizable one, say £50,000. Yes, sure if you had a huge chunk of cash, £50,000, you'd feel a lot more confident in changing your life and your way of living completely. A nice buffer, a little nest egg to get things going. No money worries for months and months right. Really? Imagine yourself now with £50,000 sat in front of you. Are you running out the door to quit work, or are you instantly upgrading your fears to the next level? How long will the £50,000 last? What if I spend too much or don't budget correctly? What if I have an unexpected large expense? What about if I spend half of it on a nice new car......? Trust me, you will soon come up with a whole new set of excuses, or poor financial ideas, why £50k isn't enough and how if only you had £100k you could do it. I can tell you from my own experience that it makes little difference and you never reach the right figure. Of course, you need to make practical arrangements for making a big life change and not be reckless, but we will talk about later in more detail in part two of this book.

One thing I can tell you though is that, right now, I have more money in my bank than I ever had when I worked and I feel no better or safer than I did before. I feel no 'richer' and I am no more relaxed about my spending habits. It has made no difference to me emotionally whatsoever, despite having reached my own phycological 'magic number' on my bank statement. The money itself has changed nothing for me. The process, the change in view, the different way I now live my life is what has changed for me. So, I can say from experience, that other than having a practical buffer for this exercise, there is no truly magic figure that will make this part of the fear go away, so you may as well write it off as just that…fear. The same core fear that stops you from making the jump for many other so-called legitimate reasons. It's manufactured, it's fake and it will never be enough. The same stands for all other excuses you have fabricated in your mind that I couldn't pre-empt, it's just your fear and self-doubt calling the shots.

What we will do now is have another go at the exercise. Go back to your answers and simply ask yourself this question…. Is there truly an answer that I can *realistically* achieve, that will honestly make me feel less fearful of making a great change to my life. Write down the 'answer' to all your fears on the page. 'I don't have enough money saved'. Well write down how much you feel would be enough to quell that fear. 'My kids are still too young', Fine, put an age that you think you would be more comfortable with. Once you have completed that exercise take a good long look at the list and then work out the practicalities of how you will achieve each answer. So maybe your figure has dropped second time round and you put down a £10,000 buffer in savings. Well work out how long it will take you to get it. A long while right? And do you feel any better now you have this 'plan'? My guess is the answer will be no, because I've already told you the fear does not go away until the jump is done anyway, so siting in the plane with £10,000, £20,000 or whatever it is, is not going to make you any less fearful of jumping out of it right? Worse than that though, look at how long it is going to take for you to achieve those answers! Look at how long it will take to save your magic buffer of savings, how old your kids will be. Work out how long it will take you to learn that magic skill you think you need, or to get that qualification. Before long you are looking down the barrel of anywhere from five to twenty years. And the reality is that 1) you won't do it anyway because things will change and 2) even if you do get there, you will have a whole other set of fears and blockers that will be bigger and will stop you anyway once you achieve these magical solutions. From this realisation you can now understand that there are no right answers to these questions, the time is now as much as it was a year ago as much as it is next year, it makes no difference. It's just about taking the practical steps. If, however, you want to kid yourself and the answer is that there is an amount of tangible money, an age for your kids, a certain level of training that you can achieve that will make me feel better, then just as good. Specify it as much as possible, write it down, and spend all your spare time achieving it before moving on with the book. Trust me though, when you have that cash, or your kids are grown, or whatever it is, you will either be too old to bother, or your answers would have changed, and you won't be any less or more ready. There is ***nothing stopping you*** other than breaking down your barriers and taking steps to make the break.

4. What if I 'fail'?

Fear of failure. Another area where we all struggle at times. What happens if after all this change you choose the wrong path, or invest your time in the wrong products or industry? What if you regret leaving your job, or need to get another one later on and can't? Very powerful questions, some of which we have just covered from your timing list, and likely similar to many more of those running around your head right now. The truth for me is that in the last few years since I left my career, I have failed numerous times. Lots. And I will continue to do so. The big difference for me now though is that I am ok with it. Perhaps more importantly…. I expect it. Writing this book for instance. I've never written before; I don't really know what

I'm doing and perhaps you might be the only person to ever read this. Should this stop me from trying? Should this stop me from completing the book and putting it out there? Of course not. Yet, for many of us it does, and perhaps five or six years ago it would have stopped me. The potential for failure. This is natural and in fact required for us to grow as individuals. Do you not make mistakes at your job? Have you not had failures at work? We all have and all will continue to do so. The difference for me now is I try and ensure I see them as opportunities for growth and not a reason to berate myself, or have a month-long regret and anxiety episode. Nobody is really able to achieve much without taking risks, trying new things, and in turn accepting some level of failure. Failure is a form of growth. Don't confuse failing with making mistakes though. Mistakes come from poor judgement, bad decisions, and excess emotions. Failure comes from trying new things and stretching boundaries. Failure comes from being brave and making ourselves uncomfortable, looking for new and exciting things to create. Failure is our fuel to be brave, to expand and enhance our lives. Failure is to be one of your many new friends.

I will be honest and admit that being more comfortable with failure was not always easy for me and was a long journey for me to change. It will likely be the same for you. When I 'worked' for a living I always felt very much under scrutiny. I touched earlier on the pressure of performing at work, caring too much about what others thought. The constant struggle, striving to do well to continually grow and get promoted/earn more money. We have already determined this is a symptom of having a career when you are not the sort of person who is happy in one. The basic upshot is that I cared *way* too much about what my boss, my team, and everyone else at work thought. This is why you probably, as I did, have a much bigger issue with failure than is healthy to do so. I'm sure you can think of a recent situation where you messed up a report, broke something, failed to meet a deadline, anything….it may not have even been entirely your fault. Yet I expect it left you feeling full of regret, deflated, and probably experiencing some degree of disappointment in your ability. Some people are naturally better than others at coping with this, but generally those like us who don't fit in the 'normal' working world can often have a heightened fear of failure, and also often take 'blame' for natural occurrences in the working world. This is generally due to things being somewhat out of our control, and our perception of how much other people judge us, or how much we care about others' opinion. People make mistakes, you sometimes aren't quite on your game, other people sometimes don't do what they say they would for you. There are lots of natural phenomenon that can lead to a failure.

What I very quickly learned when I was running my own life is that there are *lots* of opportunities for failure and I guarantee you there will be failures for you. But as I mentioned above you must now understand the huge difference between failing and making a mistake. Failure is a clear indication that you are trying new things outside of your current capability and capacity, particularly when you have just left your place of work and have started working in a completely different way. This is the only way we grow, or discover new ideas, or 'create' new things. We fail at something, we try again, we learn, we grow. Making mistakes again and again is different. Its misguided, a repeated attempt at something that you have been unable to do before. A repetition of something that you expect to give you a different result. Courtesy of Einstein '**Insanity is doing the same thing over and over and expecting different results**'…..your job for instance?! You are already making a mistake doing your job, which is why we are here still, and you haven't put down this book. If you are miserable and unhappy in your job and have been for years, what do you actually think is going to happen tomorrow to change that? What magical miracle is going to come along and fix everything so you have a happy and fulfilling life in this job you have already hated doing for so many years? Do not carry on kidding yourself. The answer is nothing is coming along to save you. The only opportunity you have is to save yourself from making more mistakes.

Let's look at an example to help us understand further the difference between failure and making mistakes. Do you remember when you learnt to ride a bike? Most people have some minor recollection of this at least, or in fact have been lucky enough, like me, to be the teacher of such a life affirming task to a child. (In the unlikely event you haven't ever learnt to ride a bike, you can still understand the concept I'm sure, so it is still relevant). In either scenario, teacher or pupil, did you, or your child, just get on the bike and cycle off into the sunset? No, you fell off. A lot! But you got back on and tried again….and again..and again….and slowly got better and better at understanding what needed to be done and the pitfalls of riding (like slamming on your front brake). Now when you were learning yourself, did you feel as if you failed during this? I suspect so yes. Many people have strong memories from childhood of learning to ride their bike, it seems to be one of those life affirming things we all remember. There would have likely been tears, frustration, refusals and tantrums each time you went to try again. Yet the majority of us have done it at some point and achieved a positive result through continued failure to succeed at riding the bike. Now, looking from the outside, if you have taught someone (or even if you could imagine teaching someone now you have done it) how did you feel then, for them? Do you see failure when the child falls off the bike and gets back on? No, you see persistence, courage, someone willing to persevere to get to their goal. The same as I'm sure your family or friends did when they taught you. The failure we see in ourselves is simply the personal view on the situation, not the outward reality of what is actually happening. And the reality for 100% of children is that they get on a bike and at first, they 'fail'. Despite this, they end up learning to ride a bike and never forget for the rest of their lives.

Now, what if you tried a few times, or you tried to teach your child and either of you gave up? You or they would potentially never ride a bike. How would you see this then? A mistake? The mistake comes from not doing the work, not doing the job, not experiencing the failures. Failure is inevitable, failure is required, failure is needed in order to achieve. Don't resent it, don't fear it, embrace it like watching a child learn to ride a bike. The mistake is not failing in order to learn to achieve the goal. Accept it is going to be a part of your life as much as it has done in the past, but instead use it as a tool for change rather than a blocker. There is nothing wrong with you if you feel anxiety, sadness or shame when you fail to achieve a goal. Instead of trying to supress these emotions, use them to fuel your drive to do better next time, or to make changes to improve the outcome. Get back on the bike! It is impossible to avoid failure. I have said before, you are going to fail numerous times when you make big changes in your life and look to live life differently. Do not see it as defeat. As you move forward with these changes in your life do not get stuck focusing on the failures, the things that went wrong. Use the lessons for sure, but living in the past has done you no favours up to now and I can guarantee will not miraculously change its usefulness to you in the future. You can find great sources of inspiration from failure, learn lessons, and it can drive you forward and make your next goal an achievement to be proud of. Nothing worth having in life is easy to achieve.

5. Pay cheque addiction

I don't use this title lightly. Addiction is a strong word, but it is apt for the situation you currently find yourself in and this is potentially one of the biggest blockers for most people when it comes to making the jump. Why? Because it is the core fuel that keeps your hamster wheel running. It is your job 'drug'. It is what keeps you coming back for more and what gives you short term highs for what you produce at your job. It is the secret weapon that is used to keep the majority of the population nicely lined up like hamsters, being good little boys and girls, doing as they are told. You have become used to it, you have become numb to its effect, but it is with you as a constant reminder of the trap you are in. It is both your security blanket and your shackles. From my own experience I found that as my career developed and I became more financially successful as I moved from role to role, it became more obvious to me that it was more of a weight *on* my shoulders than off of them. Even as I got to the 'peak' of my old career I used to refer to the renumeration I received as a pair of ***golden handcuffs***. I felt well and truly shackled to my company. I was uninspired by my job, didn't want to do it, but there was a fat cheque at the end of every month to shut me up. Despite not being happy, I knew I was in the top few percent of earners in the country and just hated myself because I didn't feel grateful for it. Because of my own experience of the hamster wheel, the money I was paid was something that developed great value to me and that I felt I had worked and sacrificed so much for. Yet it was equally cripplingly restricting to my personal growth and development of an alternative way of living. It may not be that you feel exactly the same as I did, or you may be in various stages leading up to it, but it is highly likely that you feel 'attached' to your pay cheque in some way, and therefore ***bonded to your job***. You likely feel it is a partnership that provides you with what you 'need' yet restricts you making changes to what you 'want'. You will have some kind of opposing forces pulling you in different directions. The reality is though that this is another fabrication we are taught to believe and the truth is the opposite. The money gives you what you ***think*** you want, because you don't yet realise there are options to actually get what your body and mind ***really*** want. Go back to our principle of making mistakes and repeating the same task expecting different outcomes. How long have you disliked your job, or felt unfulfilled? Likely for years, yes? Yet you continue to do the same thing, every day, in hopes that 'one day' things will be different. Oh, and its ok because you get paid to do it yes? Well no, because you are selling your hopes, dreams and aspirations for that monthly drug because you have not had the strength to understand it will ***never*** change unless you do something about it yourself.

What makes this situation even worse is a well-known fact that 99% of the working population, particularly in western countries, live a lifestyle extremely close to their income. You may be one of the lucky ones who save a few hundred pounds or so a month for a rainy day, but I think it is unlikely. What is more likely is that you have a mortgage, car payments, bills and a whole host of other direct debits and regular bills that coincidentally make up nearly 100% of your monthly income (or in some cases, slightly over 100%). This is in fact actually ***not*** a coincidence. It is not blind luck that you can just about afford your mortgage or your rent, or you can just pay your bills and feed your family, while saving furiously for your yearly holiday. It is human nature to do so. It is you stretching the limits of your "reward", your consumption. ***You are addicted to your pay cheque.*** You are taking all of the drugs (money) that fall into your lap, and like any addict, you want more, and more……and more. Think back to your first job and the salary you had and compare it to your current one. A big difference I suspect. I also suspect that if you offered that young impressionable person the salary you are currently on, they would have thought they had won the lottery. That's because they were at the start of their journey and had not got caught up in the ever-growing cycle of consumption. So, let's see where that nice big pay cheque gets you. Let's say for arguments sake you have a very successful job and earn £50k a year, well up in the top 10% of earners in this country. Let's also say that you go in to work tomorrow and your boss decides to give you a 50% pay rise. Obviously not going to happen, but let's use this as an extreme example. On the face of it I bet you would be smiling and thinking 'Oh yes, happy days!'

We will keep things simple and assume no pension contributions or any other contributions other than tax and national insurance (based on 2020/21 tax calculator):

£50k will net you approximately £3,137 a month

£75k will net you approximately £4,345 a month

Difference in salary: £1,208 a month or £14,496 a year.

Now on paper this is an extremely tempting proposition that I am sure you would be *incredibly* happy about this. The reality is though even if you are lucky enough to be earning £50,000 a year, it will likely take a huge proportion of your working career, if not your entire career to get to £75,000 or even close to it. But let's assume you have done the grafting and paid your dues and made it to that nice senior management role. Initially you would be sitting pretty with an extra £1,208 disposable income in your pocket each month which would be lifechanging right? Well, not necessarily. What if I then came back to you a year or two later. Where would things likely be then? I can make a pretty accurate prediction. It would be highly likely that I found you in a *slightly* larger house with a *slightly* nicer car and you would tell me about your *slightly* nicer holiday you went on last year. However, you would also tell me that you didn't have much more disposable income than you used to have left at the end of each month, and it would be highly likely you would be hankering for another pay rise. Why is this though? Because it is simply human nature when in the hamster wheel to consume what we have in order to reward ourselves. Those shiny phones, inspirational car adverts and catchy jingles aren't there to make you feel good. They are there to make you aspire to spend more and to make you think you will be a better person when you have item X or Y. Don't forget for those of us in the lucky situation to earn over the living wage and not have significant money problems, any extra we have is simply disposable. It adds nothing genuine to our lives other than a requirement to run faster in the hamster wheel.

I'm sure you will agree with me that there will be two people who are reading this book right now with you, where one will earn around £50,000 a year and the other £75,000 a year, respectively. A difference of £1,208 a month. Yet I can pretty much guarantee you that those two people live an almost identical life. Sure, the one earning £75,000 *may* have a slightly nicer house (bigger mortgage) and slightly nicer car (bigger car payments), but both will be quite likely to have the same limited amount of disposable income. Their day to day lives will be almost identical. Yet the difference in salary is actually huge. The difference in their roles will also likely be significant. Both have very good jobs, but one is likely a professional with a skill (project manager, store manager, specialist craftsman) and the other is possibly a senior manager (MD of a small company, large company director). I personally know a number of people who have households that earn as much as £250k a year and the same principle is still in place. Do they have a larger house? Yes. Do they lease a nicer car? Yes. Do they have any less money worries or more disposable income on average than a professional earning £50k? Not really, no. Because like everyone else they are living within their means. Once you get past a base salary that provides you all of your real necessities like shelter, food, utilities, basic transport…the rest is just unnecessary excess. Or certainly until you get to crazy money in the multi-millions. The rest just goes on increasing the speed of the hamster wheel. You need to start being more honest with yourself when it comes to salary. As much as £25k a year extra is a lot of money (and many people struggle to live on way less than that in total). Please do not take what I say as dismissive of anyone with money troubles, I am just using an extreme example as an illustration of what major changes to your life would it mean if you were already lucky enough to be a high earner. What truly magical changes would an increase from £50k to £75k mean for you? A boat, a helicopter? No, let's not be silly, it would just provide you with more of an excuse to consume reward for your work and run faster and faster on your hamster wheel, wanting more and more. Now the median salary for 2019 in the UK was £30k. This means that on average everyone would earn that if you took all the money earnt and divided it up. It also means that as a ***minimum*** (depending on wealth disparity, which is high) ***half*** of the population live on less than that. Furthermore, approximately four million people in 2019 in the UK were unfortunate enough to live on much less than that and genuinely struggle to pay for all they need. So, in perspective, the reality is you need a relatively low base level of income to actually get what you need, the rest is just for feeding your wheel. If you used the same principle of the pay rise above and took someone who earned £16k a year and gave then £24k a year, then you ***would*** be making huge changes to their lives, because they are still at the point that they have unmet needs and can increase their base comfort. It would vastly improve their life.

This conveniently takes me back to a discussion we had earlier about how much you really want something. We discussed earlier the principle of missing out on a promotion and whether you actually really wanted it, or you just used the world around you and the 'done to attitude' as an excuse as to why you didn't get it. Do you remember we discussed having talked to all the right people, spent hours on your applications, applied for similar roles outside the company, applied and applied at every opportunity? Well, the exact same principle applies here. Unless you are a below average earner on less than £30k a year, you are addicted to your salary and it will require great effort to withdraw from it. You are going to have to make sacrifices if you want to change your life. Now I'm not saying you are going to need to sell your house or downscale to a one bed flat for your whole family. I still have the same house and same mortgage I had when I left work but what I am saying is you can't expect to make an immediate transition from pay cheque to an alternative way of funding your life without any changes or sacrifices if you already earn a good salary. It will depend on whether you really want to do this, and whether you are willing to make at least some temporary sacrifices to put the change in place. We will discuss the practicalities of this and how to prepare for this change in the second part of this book.

6. Past Investment and Sacrifice

Do you ever think to yourself that if you were to give up on your career you may have wasted all the time and effort you put into it so far? Do you think that it would be like starting all over again? Perhaps there is lack of willingness to 'throw away' all of the pain and effort and heart ache you have been through to get as far as you have? Or perhaps there is another underlying fear that you will just be 'giving it all up' to go back to square one.

I had many thoughts like this and it was extremely hard for me to eventually realise that this is another part of the 'veil' that often stops us from making change in our lives. I felt very strongly that by the time I was in my late thirties, I had already given so much of myself to develop my working career. I had sacrificed much of my true self and my beliefs to fit in to the system and get where I had got to. I had trained hard in the field of project and portfolio management. I had qualifications, I had a good reputation, and a wide range of experience. I felt that maybe I should just hang on in there and see it through? I had a ridiculously hard time seeing that it could be any other way. I had been dedicated to developing myself 'professionally', had worked hard to prove myself ready for promotion on a regular basis, nurtured difficult relationships at work, slowly built up my salary…so many things to keep progressing my career. I would always make sure it was 'moving in the right direction'. If you remember we discussed earlier one of my less pleasant experiences, being let down on promotion and side-lined and how it hurt me. Many of us have these experiences over the course of the years that we work in a job, and these cumulative feelings can leave us feeling as if we have fought a war. Would it not be natural to feel that by 'giving in' and waving the flag we are surrendering halfway through a battle? And yes, this is what it can feel like in a very real and painful way. For me, it was the feeling of defeat against those individuals who I had specific issue with. Those who I thought had been giving the 'done to feeling' to me. I felt that I was almost letting them 'win' by leaving. The first thing I need you to understand about these types of feelings is that they are completely natural and if they form part of your barrier then it is not a unique problem. I for one have shared with you that it was a huge barrier for me, and I know there are many others out there who similarly, will have them forming one of their core barriers to making the jump. Remember in Chapter One I assured you that you and I are no different? Let me also assure you that I know very well the intensity of some of the pain that one can feel about the effort and self-sacrifice you put into a job. Please do not read this and think, 'Yes it's all very well, but he doesn't really understand how much of myself I have sacrificed for my career, how strong my feelings of attachment are for this sacrifice'. I *do* understand. I understand because I tell you right here and now that I gave nearly everything I had, everything I was, to my career before I left it behind. I said at the start of this book and I genuinely meant it, that I would have been one of the last people I thought would break away from their career. Yet here I am and as before I am your living proof that I have done what we have both perceived at one time as the impossible.

Easy for me to say on paper? True, but I'm also going to follow it up with a true reflection of my experience, and what I have learnt since, about the person I built during my career and how I adapted that person to be the one I am today.

I am several years now into my alternative journey for work. In my experience, I can tell you that about 99% of what I use now to be successful in this new way of life, has been ***directly*** taken from prior experience in a role within my career. I literally can think of barely a handful of things I have experienced or achieved during my job career, that I would now say are of no use to me. Surprised it is such a small amount? I can tell you that nearly ***everything*** you have done and experienced in your working career has had a direct impact on the person you have become and the skills you hold within you today. You just aren't applying them in the right environment, nor do you realise that you can. You have the tools, you have the knowledge, you have the experience, you just don't have the right place to use it. All of the times that you have solved problems, dealt with difficult relationships, absorbed the stress and delivered to a difficult timeline. *All* these times, every one of them, you have used your core capabilities and experiences to get through it or to deliver against the odds. Your ability to negotiate, your ability to plan, your ability to problem solve, your ability to overcome obstacles. Your ability to write, to listen, to speak, to stand up for yourself. You have ability! The fact you have applied your ability to writing insurance documents, project plans, running a factory, building furniture, stacking shelves, whatever it is, that is not who you are or what you can do. You must understand there is a difference between what you are able to produce in your career orientated job, compared to your base capabilities and experience as a human being.

Take a favourite of my own from my job as head of service. This was the production of a 'quarterly business report' that I had to do, strangely enough, four times a year. As a senior manager it was my responsibility to produce a quarter yearly business report with specific measurables and performance indicators that would be shown to the Executive Directorship to show them how fantastic everything was. I was responsible for this for just over 3 years. Every quarter, without exception, it was a complete nightmare. I worked tirelessly to gather the information and translate it to an easily digestible, visually inspiring masterpiece of how well we were performing. It was my greatest responsibility as Service Head and was also my greatest cause of stress. It had me in hot sweats every three months as it rolled into view. I would have to beat the rest of the management team with a metaphorical stick to get their data. Then I had to 'massage' it to make some kind of sense and appear to be positive news. Then I had to make it look all nice and pretty in an easily digestible format for the Executive Director. What I considered to be a complete waste of my time for 3 years now benefits me in ways that I apply *every* day in working for myself. Not the ridiculous report itself....but my tenacity to get things done to quality and to time, my ability to negotiate with individuals to get things I need, my ability to condense complex information into easily recognisable data, my ability to present professional looking documents for presentation. These are all great and useful things. What was the only part that really seemed a waste of my time and effort? The fact that I had to apply my skills to making a quarterly business report. I never have since made one and I can damn well tell you I would never make another one again until the day I die, even if I was completely destitute. I can easily see now that what I have bought forward with me from my career was always there. It never left, it never changed, and it was developed because I did what I did. It's the human experience. So, whatever you have done, whether it is a quarterly business report, managed a team of workers, or you've produced a physical product in a factory, your ***ability and experience*** learned from this is what will never leave you, and what is of greatest value to you. It can't be taken away from you, and if you choose to change your life, will be with you all the way.

Take this thought pattern and apply it to your own experience. Write down the core ten to fifteen functions that you perform in your workplace. Then for each one think of what capabilities you use to perform those tasks. Core abilities, not mindless outputs that happen to be the actual job in hand, but tangible skills you have developed throughout your job. If you use my experience as your example, you will find that you are able to list a good number of capabilities within yourself that are ***not job related***. It is highly likely that less than 10% of what you list will be directly related to the completion of the function itself. You may ***think*** you are just an insurance specialist, or a factory worker, like I thought I was ***just*** a programme manager. Yet it is such a small part of who you are and what you can achieve. It is simply one area of applied capabilities and experience.

You *can* do what you want, it is yours to take, you as a person do not disappear just because you are no longer in a titled job. I reiterate, your capabilities and experience cannot be taken away and they will follow you wherever you go. Your investment and sacrifices at work have built this capability and made you who you are today. Your job has given you the strength, tenacity, and skills you need to apply yourself in any environment. Leaving your career does not mean leaving yourself behind. Quite the opposite, it means leaving the useless stuff behind with those it works for, and bringing just the good stuff to keep for yourself. You are so much more than your job.

Think of it another way, if you were hit by a bus tomorrow, how bad would things be at work? How long would it be before you were replaced? I used to think I was irreplaceable with the sacrifices I made in my role and the stress I took upon myself. Turns out within a couple of weeks I think they basically forgot I was ever there. The same will be true for you, because it is the truth that there is very little left behind. The other factor that can cause you to feel that much will be lost when leaving your job is the way you may perceive your ***personal value***. Personal value is what value you place on yourself. I am going to make the assumption, given where we are now in our conversation, that your judgment of your current personal value is relatively low. I'm also going to assume that this 'value' is more than likely to be based around what you get ***paid*** at the moment. You may or may not believe that you are worth what you get paid. You may think you deserve to be paid more on the one hand, or you may feel that you are a phony and not worth a penny on the other. A form of imposter syndrome, where you spend part of your life 'panicking', waiting to be found out and the other half feeling like you have been screwed over. In fact, you may be much like me when I was holding down a salaried job and feel both of them are true at any given point. Yet regardless of the way you currently value yourself, it is still likely to be a simple monetary one. It makes sense. Firstly, it is what you are paid so you assume someone else also values you that way but also, it is a tangible thing that you can use to reward yourself with as part of the cycle. This is why you 'work' for a living. You work, you output, you are rewarded, you repeat. The Hamster Wheel. Many people that are 'trapped' in their job or career find themselves directly tying their self-worth to their job. This can be a very dangerous and debilitating situation, as I have experienced myself. A' job-centric' identity binds you to any success or failure within that role. This is what then reinforces the hamster wheel trap as you are unable to distinguish between yourself and your job. You as a person become defined as a whole by what you do and how you perform at work. To move forward you must change your frame of mind to get you to the position where the value you place on yourself is not based on money, but on what you *create* and who you *impact*. What you can give to the world, what you can give to your friends and family, what are, or could be the 'things' that make you feel good when you do them. This is at the core of making the move to a better life outside of the shackles of a 'job' and in turn vastly improving your personal value judgment and your prospects for a 'successful' life. This is not an easy task and one that takes time, but just being aware of it at this early stage is enough to help bring courage to you to make the changes and realise that there is no real 'sacrifice' to be made.

Summary

We have covered a lot in this chapter and introduced many concepts. In order to move on from these blockers, as well as emotionally conquering them, your attitude will need to change to the way you run your own version of the hamster wheel. You will need to shift from the *consumption*-based role within the hamster wheel, to an emphasis on the ***creation*** aspect. Then it becomes a reality that the ***reward*** aspect of your new way of life comes as a 'coincidental output' of what you do. Any money or 'reward' will always ultimately come as a function of your valued creations once you change your mindset to creating things that are of value to you (and to others) as a person. By simply shifting your emphasis to creating things that have meaning to you, you are able to use your capabilities and experiences for 'good'. More importantly, rather than destroying your soul, your mind, your beliefs, it has the complete opposite effect and begins to rebuild them. I will talk more in detail about my own examples of this in the second part of this discussion, but for now we will simply focus on the theory. Does it not make complete sense to you that if you find yourself working in an environment that makes you feel valued, you find exciting, you find stimulating, doing things you love to do……. then your performance would be a significant magnitude better than when working in a job that you don't want to do?

Think of something simple right now as an example, such as a pleasurable hobby. Be it gardening, stamp collecting, sporting pursuits, gaming, whatever it is. Now think if you could apply the 40+ hours a week you currently work in your job to instead doing that thing you love. Forget about money, or applying it to a business for now, just simply think of the physical task itself and imagine you are in a position to do that instead of working in your current role. How do you feel? Excited, content, exhilarated? Also think of the ***quality*** of what you would do. If you could assign all of your time to tasks you are 1) good at 2) enjoy and 3) can continuously improve on! It would be amazing right? Further imagine how you would feel about yourself and how your personal value judgement might change. It is natural that by doing things we like doing we feed our mental and physical being with positivity, rather than negativity and this can be an extremely powerful tool in changing every aspect of our lives.

The other huge positive of an improvement in our self-worth is the effect it has on the people around us. I have never spent so much time with my wife and son, nor have I had as a good a relationship as I have at the moment with both, and this only came about because I changed the way I lived my own life.

Now I have built you up, I am going to bring you down a little. Although it is entirely possible to move on and do things you love to do instead of 'work a job' for a living, there are some limits! If your favourite hobby is sitting in front of the TV eating popcorn, then we are going to struggle a little to use that to create things of quality that bring value to both yourself and to other people, for your new way of life. That said, anything is possible and who knows, you could become the newest TV critic on YouTube….

Just remember anything is possible; great things come from passion, and most importantly your personal value judgment ***will not*** and ***has never been*** improved by producing your job-based outputs.

Chapter 4. So what do I do now……?

I tell you exactly what now. ***Personal accountability***, utilising your capabilities and experiences, and changing your view of self.

We have discussed in detail the main blockers that are stopping you when you look to change your life and shift to a different way of living. We have determined the perfectly natural and human barriers we can create for ourselves and how it is not a unique situation, nor is it one that is impossible to break through. I have explained to you my own real experiences and how the barrier turns out not to even exist once we breach it. You now know I have done it and I know you can too.

Before we look at the practicalities of what needs to be done in Part Two of this discussion, we need to conclude how we finally make the jump, when the practical changes have been put in place and prepared. I have already told you I can't *make* you do the jump. But what I hope will make the difference, is what we have been through together so far in this conversation. That I have shown you there is no magic solution and that you realise you can follow in my footsteps by simply making that one brave step. The only part you will need to do all by yourself is that one second decision of the jump itself. Right up to that moment and after too, you can have my support and experience to help you with whatever comes your way. I mentioned before that I would be around after if you wished and at the end of this book, I will fulfil that promise to you and welcome you to contact me. I would love to help you continue your journey after the initial changes. But right now, we need to get you in the proper frame of mind to tackle the second part of this conversation, where we give you the practical tools and make you completely ready for this.

The first of these is to now take personal accountability for yourself. I can give you my thoughts, I can give you my insight, my experiences…but the very bottom line is, if you do *not* take personal responsibility for this, you will highly likely finish this book and simply put it back on the shelf. I told you earlier that I guaranteed you I was no different to you. I hope, having described my thoughts and feelings in the first part of this conversation that many or maybe all of them have struck a chord with you and you realise that you can do this too. I have told you I was scared, I was anxious, I was worried about what was going to happen in my own journey, but I have also told you that I have come out the other side and learnt that the fears and anxieties are nowhere near as profound as you imagine. I was only able to accept those fears and anxieties by taking responsibility for that moment I decided to jump, and you have to do the same. The easiest way to achieve this is by making habitual changes that will make you responsible for what is happening. As you read and digest the second part of this book, I want you to start to plan ***choices and actions*** that fit in with making the practical changes we discuss in the next part (don't worry I will tell you when you need to do this). By making the right choices and completing the right actions, we use the practical side of the move to fulfil the personal accountability components. This will then slowly bring us round to having a different belief in ourselves, our values and our capabilities. There will be many specific actions and choices you will need to make in Part two of this book, and by being clear, direct, and consistent in them, you will in turn develop your own willingness, intent, ownership and commitment to doing more. It is the same principle as practicing an instrument. If you keep practicing and practicing the practical components of playing a musical instrument, eventually it starts to become second nature. It starts to become instinctive; it starts to be driven from your personality rather than the mechanics of what you do physically. Furthermore, it is a well-known fact and once you are already familiar with that being accountable to someone can help make you perform, even when you don't want to. Take your boss for instance. Much, if not all of what you do in your job now is based on this accountability to others. You are tasked with an output or a task by someone who is deemed as being more senior than you, and due to the nature of accountability and the potential negative outcomes of not delivering, you perform the task or create the output. The perfect example of mine we have already discussed is my quarterly business report. This report was made up of inputs from approximately a dozen very senior, very well-paid individuals. Because I actually stapled the thing together and handed it out as well as adding my own inputs, I was up to my neck in accountability for it. What you will need to do is switch this accountability to an internal focus. We spend all our working lives allowing others to make us accountable for our work or outputs, yet the key is to now hold ***yourself as your accountable partner***. Again, this is achieved through the setting of choices and actions that we make ourselves responsible for delivering. You then hold yourself accountable to deliver on those responsibilities. As you go on this journey you are going to need to be brutally honest with yourself and review your own performance as if it were someone else's. You will need to be honest and direct, because it will be all too easy to slip back into the old frame of mind or to 'slack off' once you are no longer accountable to a third party. Just remember as we get further into this journey and beyond…. if you are not reviewing your own performance and becoming self-accountable then who will do it for you?

The next area of readiness is that of knowing and utilising your capabilities and experiences. We have already determined that 99% of your capabilities are transferable to any environment. So again, as we get into the detail of making this change, have your skills and experiences at the forefront of your mind. Even if you must revert to your list you made earlier, or do a new one, be sure of what your core abilities are, what you are good at, and what you can achieve. You will be using these skills and experiences not only to help you with the preparatory phase of the jump, but more importantly, as the basis of what you are going to do in the future. I have achieved more than I could ever have imagined since leaving my job, but I know that this is as a direct result of applying my best abilities to the environment I find myself in, and finding the areas within it that feed my passion. Many self-help scenarios talk of 'niches' in these types of scenarios. I however do not like this choice of word and think the issue is deeper than just choosing a niche. The niche principle is based on the idea that you can apply your abilities and experiences to any environment so it can almost make it inconsequential as to what you do. Although this is still the basis on how we will work there is more to it than that. I believe it is *vital* that you are able to apply yourself with passion as well as best use of your abilities. Of course, there will be tasks, or even larger aspects of what you do that will not make you as impassioned as others; the principle must at all times be that you are fundamentally impassioned to work under your own accountability and take control of what you do in your life. Know your abilities and know what you love (or can learn to love), then apply those in the situations in which you find yourself.

As well as taking accountability for yourself, and knowing your abilities and your passions, you must also begin to nurture your self-belief system. This will begin when you are able to tap into your motives for what you do. At the moment your motive is based on financial reward, but your new basis will need to be based on the creation not consumption model we have discussed. From my own experience, the greatest core belief change that helped me believe in myself was that of *control*. My assessment of how much I control my own life has increased vastly and I have a much stronger belief in myself than I did when I was working in a job. I have a much stronger belief that I am in control of my own destiny than I ever had. But again, how do you change a core belief? You can't just change your mind? No, you do exactly as you have for the other factors we discuss in this chapter, and that is make choices and take actions that nurture that part of yourself. This belief didn't just happen for me overnight. It has taken several years of repeatable actions and smart choices that has nurtured its growth. I briefly discussed in the last few pages how I have achieved so much more than I could imagine since I left my job, and that is a fact. I have done many things I would never thought of doing (such as writing this book for one). I did this by making these *conscious choices* and taking *actions* that led me to doing those things. An example, within twelve months of leaving my job I bought a restaurant. A restaurant!? Had I any experience of owning a restaurant? No. Had I any experience of cooking in a restaurant? No. But I bought it anyway because it was one of those things I had always thought sounded fun to do (it excited me). It was presented to me in a fashion that I could apply myself to it, and I could see how I could use my skills and abilities to achieve something through it. I had it for several years and I absolutely loved it. I also made it extremely successful and sold it on as a great business. This experience is one of many others I have had that have fed my self-belief, and proved to me that I *can* control what goes on around me, and I can impassion completely new things in my life. So, make sure you maintain a goal orientated approach to the choices and action you will take, and you too will begin to build on your own self belief system.

Now before we move on to the second portion of this book, I want to ensure you are clear on where your mind needs to be and give you a tool to help maintain positive focus. We can do this with some quite simple mantras that I want you to write on a piece of paper and refer to as many times as you can/wish, as we continue down this journey of preparing yourself for the jump. Say them out loud, say them in your head, learn them off by heart, pull the page out the book and pin them on a board. It doesn't matter, but use these as your compass to keep your mind continuing in the right direction:

MANTRA 1: 'I am no different from anyone else and I can do as others have done'

MANTRA 2: 'I am not owed anything from anyone other than myself'

MANTRA 3: 'I consume more and more because I am unhappy in what I do'

MANTRA 4: 'I am allowed to be afraid. Everyone is afraid'

MANTRA 5: 'I am allowed a different opinion or belief to anyone else'

MANTRA 6: 'I decide when the time to do things is right, time does not decide for me'

MANTRA 7: 'Failure is ok. Failure is acceptable. Failure is inevitable'

MANTRA 8: 'Chasing money will never significantly change my life or improve my happiness'

MANTRA 9: 'Nothing I have done in my life has been a waste of time. I am here because of it'

MANTRA 10: 'I can change my core beliefs by repeating simple choices and actions

Part II: Activation

Introduction

If you have been able to get this far in the book then firstly congratulations! You haven't been scared off entirely. Now though, is the time for *action*. I am hoping that you now understand, and hopefully believe the base foundation we have covered. Now you can look to make the steps to a different life and join me on the other side of the fence. I pray that I have shown you enough, and explained my own experiences sufficiently, to convince you that you *are* strong enough to make the same decision that I have. This truly is achievable by anyone who wishes to do it.

As we enter the actionable phase of this transition it is highly likely that you will have moments where you worry, or feel that you are overwhelmed. ***Do not panic***! This is completely normal. Please ensure if this happens that you take the time to review our mantras, or perhaps even go back to a portion of this book that relates to your concern and re-read it. There is no right or wrong answer when it comes to changing your outlook and mental readiness, so do not berate yourself if you stumble. Just pick yourself up and get back on the bike moving slowly ever onwards, rather than taking up your place again on that hamster wheel running round and round and going nowhere. The reality from here on in, is much of the hard work is done and I encourage you to double down and go 'all in' on really working hard through these next steps. As I have suggested, and from my own experiences, this next part is actually the easier part of the transition. This is because it requires ***direct practical action,*** rather than working on our inner fears and mental attitudes. Most people find they worry about failing to provide for themselves and their family and leading a good quality of life after making the jump. The reality is that the psychological blockers are the biggest barrier and you will hopefully find, as I did, that things become a little easier from here on in. After all, much of what is coming in the rest of the book is a series of simple steps that just need to be followed.

Steps that I have *direct experience* of and steps that I can *share with you* to help you achieve your own goals.

Now despite all we have talked about, I'm sure 'money' is going to still be at the forefront of your mind, as it was for me before I made the jump. So, we will be diving into that straight away in the next chapter. It is always the first thing people ask me about when it comes to making the jump and I'm sure you just want to get straight into the detail. The first thing to make clear, however, is that each and every one of us will have *different* demands, expectations and realities when it comes to your finances. Remember our discussion about a 50% pay raise for someone on a low income vs a high income? This is always the toughest area for people to discuss practically, and often one that people struggle to be open and honest about. However, the principles will be exactly the same for you as it was for me, and for anyone else, so just follow the steps and apply it to your own situation. I will endeavour to use my own actual situation and experiences as a real-life example to give some context, but just remember that it is just that. A relevant real-world example of how it has been done before, but not exactly how you will achieve the same. Remember always though, if it's been done before ….

MANTRA 1: 'I am no different from anyone else and I can do as others have done'

One of my pet hates when it comes to any kind of course or book on working for yourself, is the authors never ***really give you any proper examples*** or 'give themselves up' to the reader. I have discussed some very personal and private matters in these pages and am happy to continue doing so, should it help someone else be able to experience what I have. I have no issue with this and I hope it will be beneficial for you the reader. Nobody ever really puts their neck out and says this is 'specifically what I did' to get where I am today. It's all smoke and mirrors. They give you directions on what to do, but never tell you if or how it works!? It's bizarre. I just don't get it. Well, I guess on one level I do…many of the self-help books and courses appear to have a thin thread of useful information and then when you actually dig into it, they leave you with little more than a few ideas. Which inevitably is why the person telling you what to do is often only really making their living from doing exactly that. 'Do as I say and not as I do!'. I firmly believe the majority of so-called self-help books and the gurus who write them, are simply about spinning a dream in order to try and make their own dreams come true. I believe its apt to use the somewhat outdated phrase here of 'those that can't do, teach'. This failure to follow through and reveal real experiences is where I always felt anything I read, or anyone I followed, fell short. This is why I'm trying to be as candid as I can and in this following section and open up on specifics of what I have done. You too will find that you also need to be much more open and honest with both yourself, and others around you. One part of this is you *will* need to develop a willingness to talk about money. I am a strong believer that openness is the key to a happy life and this works across all levels. I am *much* happier to discuss financial matters in detail with anyone, and often I find people are shocked, almost like I've walked out into the room in my undies. For instance, I have literally this week, while writing this component of the book, bought a swim spa for my garden (it's like a giant hot tub you can swim in). Some of my friends came round at the weekend and I was excited to tell them where it was going, how we were going to use it etc. I then preceded to tell them how much of a great deal I got and specifically how much I paid for it. (Incidentally it was twelve thousand pounds. Yes, a lot of money, but do I care you know now? No.) Not to show off, but because I don't care if people know! It makes no difference to me. It's like when someone says they like something new they have seen in your house and say 'oh I hope you don't mind me asking, but can you tell me how much you paid for that?'. Sure!

Why would I mind? In fact, I'll probably tell you before you ask anyway, because I love getting good deals and sharing it with people! Most people protect their own financial situation like it's a big secret, or some hugely personal thing. Sure, it is a 'private' matter as to what you do with your own money and how much you have, but it is all part of the fake show. Holding back from others what your company/boss/ thinks you are 'worth'. Most people tend to covet it as their private representation of themselves and the value they think they bring to the world. We need to help you get over this. Besides, if you are not comfortable with discussing it to at least some degree, how easily do you think you will be able to discuss with a potential customer how much you want to charge them? How easily do you think you will find it to phone someone up and chase an outstanding fee owed to you if you do some freelance work? How will you push down your supplier prices to get the best deal? You must learn to be more comfortable with your own money and finances, and be more open to it not being such a big deal or such a closely guarded secret that defines you. This in turn will allow you to be more comfortable with money in general and more comfortable with your wider self-worth too. It is not the enemy here. You will also find it begins to make it less of a 'monster' to you, allowing you to be more comfortable with your potential fluctuating financial situation, once you make the jump. It *will* be more chaotic, certainly in the beginning. Nobody is coming to rescue you and give you a pay slip at the end of the first month except you. Remember it is our addiction to money and our obsession with it that causes us these financial headaches in the first place. It will be tough to understand that you have to let go of this comfort blanket and this measure of you as a person, in order to bring about positive change. There is no cheat for this, no short cut. You *must* get your head in the space to accept that money is just a thing and it doesn't rule your life or define who you are.

As we progress through this next part of the book, and look to actually get on and start building your new life, we will cover aspects of money, self-management and practical business basics that you will need to transition into your new self-sustained lifestyle. So, let's jump straight in and start talking about getting yourself financially prepared!

Chapter 5: Financial planning and readiness

Let's get into it and deal with the big bad elephant in the room, which is preparing yourself for a pay cheque withdrawal. It is just round the corner, so we need to make sure you are ready to live your financial life in a whole different way. As it stands at the moment your whole life is based around a ***fixed*** and ***known*** amount of money that comes in to your account once a month. The way the system works for you at the moment, is small portions of that money are divided up into payments that go to pay various components of your financial life. The 'big ones' like mortgage/rent, car loans, utilities etc. Then you have a percentage left over for regular purchases like shopping, coffee, meals out, Netflix, petrol etc. Then some of you have that tiny little bit left over that goes in the savings or holiday fund or gets spent on 'miscellaneous'. If not, you probably have that tiny bit of a deficit that you carry through each month, blindly hoping that things will improve. The reality is though, you have a very rudimentary system of a monthly cycle that repeats again and again and again. This, as discussed in part one of the book, is your monthly 'addiction' that constitutes your salary and keeps you running in that hamster wheel. You need to prepare yourself that this is going to stop and things are going to be done differently. At least for the short and medium term. You are going to have to become more dynamic and comfortable with managing your finances in both a short ***and*** long-term format, rather than just this set regular monthly cycle.

The first reality check you need at this juncture is that you are ***highly likely*** to earn very little in comparison to your current salary for the next 3 to 6 months. It's just a practical reality. Like I said in the last chapter, real world here, no smoke and mirrors. It took me just under 6 months before I was truly able to see inroads into my income after leaving my job. For you it may be more, or even less, everyone will be different. But there will be a period of larger instability before it settles down more. If you are starting your own business, learning new business skills etc…whatever it is, you need time to make these things happen. So, for this reason we need to make ***provision*** for that to be a reality. If you are expecting it and are prepared for it, then it is less of a fearful process, and something you can attain some kind of control over. 'Wait!?' I hear you ask. 'didn't you say earlier in part one that there is no amount of money that I can have behind me that will make the change more likely, but now you are telling me to save money?'. No! there is a difference. Waiting around to have thousands of pounds to fund your current lifestyle for months and months is far different from accepting the reality that you *are* making the jump and you will need to have a specific plan and ***make sacrifices*** to fill the void left by your salary. The first is you just making excuses as to why you can't do it and the second is you accepting the reality that you are doing it now and actually putting in mechanisms to help you make the move. This is because the second comes with an additional component. That is, the reality that your spending habits are (again at least in the short to medium term) going to have to change. You are going to have to make these sacrifices. We have discussed this before. You can't just carry on as you have with the comfortable knowledge of your monthly income. This is the drugs talking. You need to withdraw and use money as a tool rather than as a crutch to satisfy your sadness. If it was as easy as flicking a switch everyone would be working for themselves and doing exactly what they want, when they want.

Now don't be too scared if you are in a job or a financial situation at the moment where you are unable to save your magic buffer amount of money. There are two ways to fill the gap you will have when you first make the jump, which we will discuss right now.

OPTION 1 SHRINK IT

The first is to *shrink* the hole that will be left without a pay cheque to be as small as possible. And what do I mean by this? Well, I will tell you. If you look into the future three months you can very easily calculate exactly how much money you are going to have from your monthly wage. Doesn't matter if you earn £1000 a month or £20,000 a month, same principle applies. Let's give an example that's nice and easy. Lets say you 'take home' £2000 a month from your salary. Well, very quickly we can determine that that will give you a total of £6,000 in your pocket in the next three months. It has also (unless you recently received a tremendous end of year pay rise) given you that same £6000 in the *last* three months. So, the very first thing we need to do is go back and audit that last three months of your life. And you will need to do this to the *penny*. The massive advantage tool we have for this these days is electronic banking. You should without too much difficulty be able to go on to your online banking and download the last three months of your accounts which will show every last penny that has gone into and out of your account.

Why are we doing this historically before we plan ahead? Three very good reasons:

1. You will understand exactly where your money gets spent with your current spending habits (you will be shocked!)
2. You will identify areas of expenditure that are much larger than you expect
3. We can use the data to plan ahead the next three months and shrink the gap

So, I want you to gather all this information from the last three months and then complete the following exercise:

Draft a computer spreadsheet, or use pen and paper if you don't have it. As you start from exactly three months ago (1st of that month due to normal pay cycles) I want you to start ticking off and compiling EVERY *debit* line on your bank statements and credit card statements on this list. Use five columns. The first is 'Budget Item', the second, third and fourth are 'monthly spend' (e.g month one, month two and month three) and the fifth is 'Total Spend'.

Budget item – The name of the expenditure. Be it mortgage, phone bill, car repair etc. Whatever it is, give it a title so you can go back and understand exactly what it is later.

Monthly spend – The actual amount. For some of these there will be only one entry, perhaps for mortgage or rent for instance. For others there will be many, perhaps Takeaways! For the multiples, once you have created the line, each time you come across an entry for that budget item simply add it to the total. Complete a column for each Calender month.

Spend for total period – Once you have completed this exercise for three separate months in the three columns on excel or on your sheets of paper, simply add them together and put the totals in the 'spend for total period'.

I have completed a basic example below to help if you are struggling:

Budget Item	Month 1	Month 2	Month 3	Total Spend
ROOM RENT	£ 600.00	£ 600.00	£ 600.00	£ 1,800.00
GAS AND ELECTRICITY	£ 150.00	£ 150.00	£ 150.00	£ 450.00
FOOD SHOPPING	£ 200.00	£ 200.00	£ 200.00	£ 600.00
LUNCH WHILE AT WORK	£ 150.00	£ 150.00	£ 150.00	£ 450.00
WORK TRAVEL EXPENSES	£ 60.00	£ 60.00	£ 60.00	£ 180.00
NIGHTS OUT	£ 110.00	£ 110.00	£ 110.00	£ 330.00
TV	£ 65.00	£ 65.00	£ 65.00	£ 195.00
COFFEE TAKE OUTS	£ 35.00	£ 35.00	£ 35.00	£ 105.00
FOOD TAKE OUTS	£ 50.00	£ 50.00	£ 50.00	£ 150.00
GYM	£ 90.00	£ 90.00	£ 90.00	£ 270.00
CAR PAYMENTS AND INSURANCE	£ 210.00	£ 210.00	£ 210.00	£ 630.00
PETROL	£ 40.00	£ 40.00	£ 40.00	£ 120.00
MOBILE PHONE	£ 40.00	£ 40.00	£ 40.00	£ 120.00
	£ 1,800.00	£ 1,800.00	£ 1,800.00	£ 5,400.00
SALARY	£ 2,000.00	£ 2,000.00	£ 2,000.00	£ 6,000.00
SAVINGS	£ 200.00	£ 200.00	£ 200.00	£ 600.00
GAP?				£0

Once you have completed this exercise in detail, check the difference in balance of your bank at the start of the period and at the end to see if you have saved anything. Make a quick comparison to the total on your sheet (plus any savings you have made) to the total you have calculated as your three months of salary income e.g. in the case of our example salary, if you had been able to audit £5,400 (and saved £600) of the £6,000 income, you get a gold star!. If you cannot get to ***at least 95%*** of understanding where your money goes then you need to try and fill more gaps! If you get 100% correlation you get an 'A+'.

For the next part of the exercise, you will need to rank them from highest 'spend for total period' amount (at the top) to lowest 'spend for total period' amount (at the bottom). Now you have done this you have in front of you an exact breakdown of your hamster wheel lifestyle! You have a complete transparent view of everything you have *consumed* in the last three months. And I will say with 99% certainty there will be some significant 'wows!' in there. So why don't you take a moment if you haven't already to just have a quick look down the list and see where it all goes.

How much have you spent on coffee in the last three months? How much have you spent on going to the pub, or having takeaways? How much on clothes? How much miscellaneous/unaccounted for cash or touchless payments have you made? I am convinced you will be shocked. If you are not, then great for you! You obviously are astute in understanding the use of your money, so if anything, you should find this whole exercise much easier. For the 99% though, the reason you are shocked is simple. That's because you aren't in *control* of your finances enough. You are spending money on consumption because you aren't happy in what you do for your job and you are trying to make yourself feel better by rewarding yourself. Don't beat yourself up for it, it's completely natural and normal and I have done it, as are many millions of others right this second. Million-dollar question is though are you still willing and able to make the changes to *not* do this? This is where most fail. The fear comes back, the doubt, the worry. Can I do it differently? Can I 'survive' on less than this? Yes, Yes, Yes! You are resilient, you are passionate, you are capable, you can achieve amazing things! This is nothing! This is the same fake veil of fear that was holding you back emotionally in part one of this book. You can do this if you *want* to do this. We are talking about your *one life*, your happiness, time with your family, your mental health, your self-worth…and so much more. How does that balance against some numbers on a sheet that relate to coffees, Netflix, meals out, clothes, cars, holidays…I could go on? It doesn't balance against it. It is meaningless against it. And it's not like you can't get these things back either. I said earlier I am now more financially stable than I have ever been in a job. Maybe it will be a few months, maybe it will be a year, who knows. That is nothing! And it's a onetime thing. I've done it, and I can tell you for sure I'm never going back. My reward is now having freedom for the rest of my life. Please, don't be suckered in by fear. It is just a fake manifestation to stop you from taking action. It is the built-in, made-up mechanism that keeps us running in the hamster wheel. Any moment you start to waiver at this point please again remember, I have done it…..and guess what?…

MANTRA 1: 'I am no different from anyone else and I can do as others have done'

You do not ***need*** the majority of the things you are consuming because of your job if you do not have that job. The self-rewarding, the attempts to try and elicit a happy feeling, the one upmanship of the slightly better set of clothes, or fatty takeaway…these happy feelings can be achieved through ***creation*** instead. Furthermore, is it even working?! Do you feel happier now you have that car, or watch that TV show, or wear those nice shoes? No! That is because it doesn't work. But you are still doing it. Stop! ***Right now*** is where you can start joining me. You will learn to create to fulfil your emotional needs, your passions, your dreams. And the fabulous, amazing, supercalfrajulistisexpialidociousness of this is that:

1. It makes you feel good to Create
2. When you create with passion people will want a slice of it and will reward you for it

This area is where I find my own passions and as you can probably tell I am very emotive about it. I talked very early on in the book about there being no 'secret' to quitting work and living life differently. And it's true, there is no big secret, but the closest thing to it is this concept of **fulfilment through creation and not consumption**. I literally *love* this concept and think it is practically magic. It has a double strength effect of supporting your emotional needs *and* your financial situation. If you are spending time creating with passion you are not only not spending money to fulfil your emotional needs, you are creating things out of inspiration for others to covet. Whether it's your dream to be a gardener, a stamp specialist, an artist, a CEO of your own vacuum cleaner company, it doesn't matter. Shift to *creation* from *consumption* and your life will change dramatically. Now, let's get back to shrinking that gap coming in the next three months.

So, we have our detailed list of expenditure from the last three months and we need to utilise that to *shrink the gap* for the coming three months. Firstly, duplicate the audit sheet in its entirety as we will use this to reverse engineer the next three months.

Identify *all* expenditure related to actually going to work. This may seem a little strange, but you will be surprised. I'm talking about train tickets, car parking, buying lunch, buying coffee, buying shirts, cleaning suits etc etc. All of this can be directly deleted. Gone. Instantly.

Do a first pass of all the items left on the sheet, particularly those nearer the bottom of the sheet. Your big expenditures are still likely to be mortgages, cars, loans etc, and are not the easily picked low lying fruit. The stuff near the bottom is. Be robust. Identify every item on that list that you would class as a real luxury. And I don't mean luxury yacht. I mean, clothes, takeaways, restaurant bills, cinema visits, random online orders of toilet roll holders! Anything and everything that is just a 'thing' or an 'on-the-spot' purchase where you are consuming to try to appease yourself. Take them out too, deleted, gone.

Now…Here comes the tricky and personal bit. There is going to be a large 'grey area' of stuff that you probably are going to class as 'necessary' or 'essential'. I'm talking Netflix, Sky, Apple TV, gym memberships, subscription boxes, holiday savings etc etc. These are currently the 'things' that help make your life worth living and the treats that you give yourself to reward yourself for working your job (that we know doesn't really work!). Filter just these items and see how much they constitute as a percentage of your monthly expenditure. If you are lucky and they sit at around 10% then I would say to you, unless you have not been able to shift much from the other sections, then you can probably sit pretty and leave these alone and still keep some of your little luxuries. However, if you are looking down the barrel of maybe 20% plus of your expenditure going on these, then unless you have made huge inroads into the other two sections you are going to need to sacrifice some of these.

The upshot is, you want to be looking for a minimum of 30% saving across the 3 categories for the next 3 months. 40% plus, you are on to a winner. So you may need to ask yourself how much you *really* want to quit your job, compared to having the best TV package and the fanciest gym membership. Perhaps you aren't ready to give those up, but I ask the question once more. Do they truly pay a role in your happiness? Are you happy? Perhaps there are some that longer term you do find important to your life; just remember, this is just for now. We are looking at the next three months, planned out, organised and in place, not the rest of your life. Take up running for three months, its free!

Once this exercise is completed, and you choose to remove as much as you can bare, you will have a *specific plan* of exactly what you need in terms of income for the next three month. You will have made it *shrink* by reducing the known expenditures you will take out. This can then be used to really tell you how much you will need to bring in for your first three months of living on the other side of the fence. It may be that you decide you will do 1 or 2 days freelance or contract to begin with, if this figure is high and if you are in the type of salaried profession where consultancy work is normal / acceptable. Otherwise consider doing something part-time on a short-term basis until you are fully set up to go solo. Perhaps you see it as a comfortable figure to aim for straight off the mark. The important thing is that it is now a known thing and is no longer a mysterious 'how will I feed my family?' situation. And yes it may still feel uncomfortable and may bring you some anxiety, but this is normal and in fact a good thing. Use it, use it, use it! Use it to light the fire underneath you, it gives you a goal, a purpose, a direction to go in when you start off on your journey. Remember again, I said quitting your job is not about quitting work, you must work hard. But you will be working hard for yourself and your family and I tell you now there is no motivation like it.

OPTION 2 SAVE FOR IT

Now you have hopefully identified a fair percentage of your expenditure you can cut down to reduce your financial needs for the next three months, the next option we have to build on this further if you feel it is necessary is to *save* for it. This is where you actively plan for the next three months to live without the itens you have removed from your budget while *still* working. Let me explain. As I said before everyone's financial situation is different and everyone's view on what is and isn't 'necessary' is also different. You have however at least created some kind of expenditure plan that shows you how you can live off less money in the coming months. *If* you feel the fear is too much or your anxiety levels will still stand in your way, and you want to decrease the gap further before making the jump you can simply turn this plan on while you still work! It's a very simple but effective and well thought out option. Say for instance your expenditure plan worked out you could remove £400 a month from your monthly costs. So, if you were to leave your job and do something off your own back you would only need to get whatever your salary is minus the £400 right? Sure. But what about if you put the plan in place and kept your job for a few months? Then you would have the same monthly income but be able to SAVE the £400. If we did this for three months you would save £1200. You can then add this to the bottom line of your expenditure plan when you make the jump which will mean your first three months without salary will require £800 less than what you earn *plus,* you are already used to being less reliant on consumption! Simple in principle, yes? Furthermore, it's a great way to 'try before you buy'. Have you made a plan that you can stick too? Are you really able to cut out all those luxury spends? Try it for a month or two, pretend you have quit your job but don't actually do it yet. Nobody needs to know; you can just run it as a personal stealth exercise to determine if you really can keep your self-discipline to follow the plan. And you can! You just make sure you are consistently disciplined to follow what you have put down on paper and can review it on a regular basis. It's like going for a run. You plan to do it, you go do it, you get the results. You plan to do it, you skip it (too cold, too tired, too rainy…whatever) you don't see the benefits. Same principle applies here. Test your mettle. Because if you can't be disciplined enough to do something as simple as follow a basic set of rules of 'do and do not purchase these items' then perhaps you may want to think again about the whole thing! (I'm sure that's not you…or if it is you've read an awful lot of this book to turn back now.)

So, like I said, if you are looking at not being able to dramatically reduce your expenditure plan from the audit and be comfortable at that point, you can double its efficiency by introducing it *before* you leave your job. You win by trying it on for size, as well as saving for when you actually make the jump. Yet, furthermore you can begin to wind down your commitment to your 'career' and begin planning what you want to do for the future, so you can try and hit the ground running once you do leave your job.

Chapter 6. What you *love* vs what you can *do*

Remember the earlier discussion about how people can find themselves defined by their job? Where they find themselves interlinking it throughout all aspects of their life; the failures (and successes) are all part of the deep psychological fears we have that stop us changing. The true beauty of leaving work and being your own person is that you sever these ties and it brings you to a place where there are simply no rules. Many self-help books or courses will tell you specifically things you should do to be a success, like run your own social media management empire, or become an online freelancer (yet as we know they often don't tell us specifically how). The reality is, and certainly my own reality (which I will talk in detail about in the next chapter) is that you are not fixed to *any* format. It has been one of my greatest lessons since making the jump, as much as also the biggest surprise to me. You will not believe the level of freedom you can have to try ***Anything you want to***. In fact, I encourage you greatly to remain as open and flexible as you can, particularly as your journey matures and you stabilise. Certainly, the majority of the beauty I receive from my new way of life is I literally will do or try ***all*** things that happen to come my way. Of course, I make plans and have detailed ideas of how my own business interests are going, but I make sure I never turn my back on any idea that pops into my head or that comes knocking on my door. You too will find that an unbelievable and fascinating journey begins once you have the freedom to literally do whatever you want. By this though please remember as I said in an early chapter that this doesn't mean you can just wander around 'doing what you want'. You must remember you have to work hard; this other life is not one of endless leisure!

There is, hopefully, already that dream, or passion that you aspire to or look to achieve (don't panic if not, as I didn't really have one when I started). This is always a great start when you have made the jump, but there are some things you need to understand. You need to be able to accept that doing what you love may not be something you can instantly drop sticks and do. We all have the bubble of enthusiasm about something in our life and I hope yours is large, as this really is the Holy Grail for those of us that quit work. And in fact I would suggest it is the end goal of 'quitting work well', because ultimately that is where we should end up…doing things we love. Like all things in life though there is this ***practical journey*** and a reality that working within one's passion may not be an immediate possibility. I cannot emphasise enough that you must understand that you will likely have to do things you ***don't*** want to do to start with when you quit your job and look to live life differently. If you end up taking a contract, or a temporary job, or go and work in a supermarket for a short period of time…you are doing it for a ***reason***. It is not failure and it is in fact a positive sacrifice that you are going through in order to move closer towards your dreams of living a life that you love. I will tell you more about my specific journey to this end goal in the next chapter of this book, but first we need to discuss this transitional period and how you need to be disciplined and focused.

Now if everything has gone as expected in our planning phase, we have a financial plan where we are going to close the gap, and/or save for three months before we jump. So now all we have left to do is actually come up with that money that is required, as we won't be getting paid by someone else. And for this, not a major surprise, but you are going to need to work for it! In this modern connected world is has never been easier to just pick up the phone or turn on your computer and find work right this second. Forget unemployment figures, forget stories of a hundred people applying for one job. That's all your old world, I'm taking about finding work, not finding a job (again). Now this next part where we work for it, is basically what I call the ***proving ground***. It is a place you can go to, quite quickly, with relative ease, that will allow you to begin your journey of self-sustainability. It will provide you with flexibility and income while you ***also*** build your new business, retrain, look for investment, develop your passion etc. There is a big difference between looking for work to make some money and looking for a job to make money. When I handed my notice in to my job, in fact a few days before, I contacted a project management temp agency (I had already sorted my CV in advance) and I registered to say I was able to work at anything they had that they thought was suitable. I hadn't been in project management directly for a few years since being a senior manager, but it was a skill I had and I knew could earn me money. Before I even left my role (three months' notice as senior manager) I had had two interviews for temporary contract work and had been offered one working in London for six months. The day rate was extremely good and along with my new expenditure plan I knew that I could work this contract for six months and have enough money that I would not have to get more money at all for the next six months, *if* I stuck to the plan. So, I took the contract, worked hard and in my own spare time started to develop areas that interested me. The beauty of a contract role or temporary job when you leave work is you frankly don't have to care once five o'clock comes. You have no career to protect, you have no boss to dramatically impress (long term at least). It is surprisingly liberating, and gives you time outside of the' nine to five' to actually be motivated to build what you actually want to do. Now, I know that not everyone has a readily sellable skill such as a project management background, but most people reading this book will have at least *some* kind of background skill or capability, that they can trade short term in contracting, or simply get a part time hourly job locally in. Even better, if you already have a passion or area of interest you want to get better at, then go get a job in that arena. If you want to run your own successful Gardening Company, then….well…..go get a job as a landscape labourer for a local company, or go and work in the garden section at your local DIY centre. You have to look at this part of the transition from a positive aspect of learning, of almost wrapping yourself in a cocoon, ready to emerge as a kick ass butterfly! ***There is no such thing as going backwards here.*** Don't be a snob, and don't think that anything is beneath you. So what if you had a high flying job and now take a contract in basic administration, or labouring, or box stacking? You have nothing to prove, you have no commitment, you will not owe them or anyone else anything. Take every ounce of experience you can out of it, ask questions, sneak a look at suppliers, observe how people treat their customers, how they get leads…anything and everything. You must treat this period as a necessary one to make the transition. Part of the *fear* we talked about in part one of this book that stops us from jumping, is the fact that working a job and working for yourself/having your own successful business, seem so far detached from each other. You have no idea of the journey to get there. Well, the transition period is that journey! You have two simple choices. You either take any work you can get that fulfils the financial gap you have left after your financial audit, while you work on your own passions *or* (much better if you can) you take temporary work (any work) that relates to an area that you want to spend your time in going forward. Like I said, work for a gardener if you want to be one, be a temporary office junior at a social media firm, if you want to see what they do and how it works. Stack boxes at a brewery if you want to start your own beer brand. It's really quite simple if you don't over complicate things. Temporary jobs are usually readily available. Search the web or go into a dozen local job agencies and just make it happen. After I had filled some of my financial gap with working as a project manager, I had decided (which I will talk more later) to get back into an old passion of mine which was web design. I signed up to an online job board where people posted their IT requirements. Having zero feedback and zero examples, I remember clearly the first job I took on was to fix a contact form on someone's website for the grand sum of £8. I submitted a pitch that basically said I had little experience, but was looking to break into the field again and I would work hard until I had solved their problem for them, and would be most appreciative of the job and any feedback they could give me afterwards. The reality was that I had to study in detail for several hours to fix the problem, but I did it and I got my first feedback. Three years on I have top certification on this website and my largest customer through this website has paid me more than £15k this year alone…..just one customer. I followed the simple steps of just getting on with it and putting myself out there, willing to do whatever it took to progress.

If you follow this simple plan and you focus and are self-disciplined you will find that your attitude towards this work is very different from when you had a job. You will find that you don't feel obligated, that you don't feel under pressure to perform for your end of year review, you don't need to be liked by all your work colleagues, you don't care that you may have to do something for £8! Keep yourself focused on the plan and it will become a very liberating experience. What it will also show you very quickly is how adaptable you really are, and how none of that rubbish that used to ruin your life actually ever made any difference at all. It was just there to spoil your day. Be humble and consistent in your daily activities and little can go wrong. It still amazes me what I used to put up with in my job and how so very different things are for me now. I have developed skills I would never have dreamed of ten years ago and shiver when I think of that damn quarterly business report! Looking back now, it simply looks like utter madness!

By working through this transition period, you should feel liberated from the shackles of a job and, as long as you remain focused, you can start to develop your own skills or business plans, outside of the working day. No longer should you be coming home trampled and depressed, carrying armfuls of reports or assessments that need to be done by the morning. You should be motivated, disciplined, and finish work to leave it behind and then spend all your spare time on building your new life. You will be amazed what can be achieved outside of 'working' hours when you don't feel emotionally or even physically attached to a job twenty-four hours per day. Be disciplined, work hard and develop your dreams. You will either be lucky enough to already have those dreams, or like me, you will be surprised at how they come to you as you begin. Either way you will get there and find things that impassion you in ways you cannot fathom.

Chapter 7. Understanding there is no fixed format – my example

The main purpose of this chapter is to use my own journey to try to reiterate and provide more detail to you that there literally is ***no single fixed format***. What you can do with your life once you have broken free and made the jump from having a job is basically anything. We are of course following a plan and also learning from my own experience and that of others I have helped but ultimately you are going to be creating a unique life based on your own self. It's much like we have all joined an art class, learning painting techniques. We are perhaps painting the same subject, but each and every one of the classes paintings will look and feel unique to each artist. I can't tell you enough times that what you do after making the jump will be completely and utterly unique to yourself, and rightly it should be. Your skill set, your passions, your drive, are all unique characteristics to you. We have discussed in depth that fundamentally we are the same, but here at this point is where we focus on those aspects of you that *are* individual and give you the specific detail to map out your future life. I suspect the best way to demonstrate this is to show you what I have been doing myself in the last few years since I quit work.

I promised I would be transparent….So here it is:
Worked as a contract project manager
Bought and run a bistro restaurant
Created individual wood furniture pieces
Learnt how to install liquid epoxy industrial flooring
Written a child's picture book
Opened up a pet boarding business
Been a small business advisor
Become an established online freelance web-design and graphic designer
Designed and sold digital art items online
Written this book!

Different from your last few years yes! Not only have I done all of the above, I indeed still do most of them now and have developed several of them into sustainable income streams (and I still have a number of things I want to start doing). My 'business' as such is simply a collection of services and or skills I have developed over the last few years that a) I enjoy and b) provide me income. And these are all based on me creating and not consuming. You can see they are all completely different and there is limited or no connection between writing, graphic designing and laying liquid floors! That is other than my own creativity and capabilities. You will also notice they are generally all *normal everyday things.* I have a working model that provides me satisfaction as a person as well as sustenance to lead a comfortable life for me and my family. And all of it without an secret online marketing course, or get rich quick scheme. I have indeed 'quit work well' and now have opened up exactly what I do to show you there is no secret formula or plan. I'm sure you will look at that list above and be somewhat surprised at the diversity of it and the apparent randomness of it, or indeed actually how simple it is in many ways. As I have said many times, I am unmasking the fact there is no secret! There are no secret industries, special social media advertising consultant jobs, or any other 'hidden' wonders from you on this side of the fence. All the smoke and mirrors you see on the internet of millionaire twenty-year-olds and their 'secret courses' to get you to six figure salaries in thirty days are just as they seem. Too good to be true. They are there to sell you readily available free information that they have pooled together in a nicely presented format that if you were truly motivated you could just go and find yourself. The reality is I have simply left myself open to opportunities as well as utilised my skills and passions to make a success out of not having a job. I never closed myself off from any thought, chance, or offer that came my way, and in fact I still don't. I have ideas every day and conversations every week with people about potential new things to do. This is a *very* exciting place to be and provides me with a great feeling of accomplishment. In fact now I have written that list and look at it, I smile, as I simply can't believe it myself. Me, Jo Bloggs, Mr Smith, a 'normal' regular guy has broken the mould and knocked it out the park. So please let's do the same for you!

To talk a little more about my own journey for context, my contract work at the top of this list is clearly my transition period and one that worked well for me. It was well paid, it was temporary and I had prior skills to fulfil the requirement. Don't be hung up though on your most recent skills and finding work that ends up just feeling like a temporary version of the job you have just left. This can keep you in your old 'work mode' and will stifle your ability to break out and try new things. I actively encourage you to at least separate yourself to one degree from your current job when looking for your first transition role. Maybe look back to a prior role you had a few years ago, or even your first career you went into when you were young. Maybe even revert back to what you were good at, at school or college. Tutoring perhaps in a foreign language. Or if not and you want a clean slate, or lack any obvious ideas, just pick something completely different that will simply utilise your core personal strengths. I hadn't been a project manager for several years, so it at least felt somewhat alien to me when I started to do temporary PM work. I still had the base skill set and with little to no effort of reading up on current practices through the odd evening I was able to hold my own and gain a role in central London. Obviously, the perfect situation is a preferred choice of work here with something that relates to what you want to do mid and longer term. You may be like I was, however, and not have such a clear idea of what you want to do with your new life. I touched earlier on the fact that you may not have a true passion for something, nor may you have a dream of running or owning a certain type of business. In reality this doesn't really make much difference, because you can base your transition journey on your core skills and strengths. This isn't a problem. Yes, it's great if you are dedicated to starting your own gardening firm, accountancy practice, business consultancy, ice cream company etc, but you don't *have* to know that at the start. Don't let that be yet another blocker to bring up the fear and stop you from making the decision to make the change. Separate yourself from your job by at least one degree though and just begin the journey. This isn't a deal breaker. As you can see from my own example, I actually do a number of things now as I have developed several small business streams, so definitely don't feel you have to just throw yourself into one thing. Several of the key things I do now I literally knew nothing about, nor did I have even the tiniest of inklings that I would be involved in them when I first jumped and entered my transition phase. Equally I now also have nothing to do with any project management or corporate leadership, which were arguably my 'transferable skills' from my career.

The beauty of no rules is that equally you may know, and want to jump straight into something. You may know exactly what you want to do and you may want to just do that. This is great if you do and please go full throttle and get going. Remember, there is no right or wrong answer here. The important thing is developing things that you will enjoy doing. This is to make sure it fits into the creation vs consumption model and you actually will want to do it. Yes, you may not know what those areas of enjoyment are, but you can and *will* eventually find them, as I did.

Having contracted for a very short period of time I found myself able to get into the mindset we discussed in the last chapter of not feeling obligated to the role. I would find myself finishing work and switching straight into 'self' mode. No worries of what the next day would bring, what my boss thought, what outputs I needed to produce to perform for the company. I knew that I could just up and leave whenever it suited me and this was a powerful thing. Why? Because it allowed me to focus on myself and my goals. I was much happier, much more focused and spent much more of my free time exploring opportunities that interested me. This is where I came across the second item on the list, the bistro restaurant. I happened to be visiting family down by the coast and during a walk we stumbled across the closed property with a sign on the door saying up for sale. Although I had no experience in the industry at all, it had always been something, like many, that I had always thought would be exciting to be involved with. So, because I was in a more self-focused and open frame of mind, I did not feel the normal fears and anxieties that stand in our way when we are chained to the responsibility of a job. Instead, I felt excited, motivated, interested to explore it further. Long story short I partnered with my father in-law as a joint venture and we took it on! I ran it directly myself for just under three years and then sold it on as a popular ongoing business. Initially we had no idea what needed to be done. I still laugh at the first day we opened, myself and my father in-law went down to the bakers to buy cakes and bread for the lunchtime business. As the baker asked us what we wanted it suddenly dawned on us that we had no idea how much bread we would need. 1 loaf? 5 loaves? 100 loaves?! I can't actually remember how many we bought, but that doesn't matter anyway, what matters is we made a choice and just did it. Very quickly we learnt what our customers wanted and within a couple of weeks were amazingly good at putting in accurate orders for our fresh food. And this was with ***zero prior experience***. Incidentally, if you are thinking of buying a restaurant or a coffee shop as part of your 'dream' I will tell you now you will never work so hard on any other business as you will for that (but it is very satisfying). And from there it was pretty much more of the same thing when it came to looking for new ideas….web design was something I had enjoyed in my youth, so I rekindled my passion for that, the epoxy flooring was something I saw randomly on an internet video one day and thought it looked amazing, so I booked myself on a course and can now do that, while the pet boarding business came about because we couldn't find anywhere of quality near to us to board our own pet while on holiday. It was in fact my son who I think was about eight at the time who suggested we could have our own pet hotel! My wife and I decided there was a potential gap in the market and the rest is history (growing year on year and a very viable business).

You can clearly see its fundamentally actually a very simple process. If you remain open to ideas and suggestions that appear around you and you are willing to work hard at putting ideas into place. Have some faith in making decisions, then there are opportunities around every corner. Don't cower away from opportunities that the universe presents to you because you have no experience either. I have said before, it is your capabilities that will support you. I knew nothing about running a restaurant, but did it. I knew nothing about running a small pet boarding business, but did it. Every one of my current streams, bar web design, have all been new experiences for me. Also please don't now doubt that you will be the one person who *can't* ever find opportunities or good things never happen to. As I keep saying to you, I'm not special, I didn't have any particularly expert skill at identifying opportunities or business ideas. I didn't have a huge network of friends or contacts from work to kick start my ideas. If anything, due to my social struggles I had less than average contacts. You absolutely have the same capability as anyone else to choose to open yourself up and be flexible to new ideas and experiences. In many ways people often try to look too hard for that one amazing, untapped secret, which as you now know isn't there! This is why they never make their move, because they concentrate on the woods and miss the tree right in front of their face. Remember to not try too hard, but also don't over think the idea, as again you will begin to talk yourself out of it, or convince yourself you won't be able to do it. The simple fact is that I know you will have the capability to adapt to anything as long as you work hard and remain focused on changing your life.

Chapter 8. Take Control

Along with your new found attitude to embracing change and the potential opportunities that surround you every day, you will need to seriously up the self-discipline when you come over to this side of the fence. We have already discussed this, but one of the very few benefits of having a job is you are ***accountable*** to a third party outside of yourself. Be it your boss or the company itself, when you have a 'real' job, you have an accountable person to whom you are required to output for, and there are generally consequences when you don't. Be it a red-faced angry head of department in the corridor, a poor end of year review, or even the ultimate embarrassment of being sacked, you currently have an outside party that has certain 'requirements' for you to fulfil. It is a little ironic too that this part of having a job is often the part people believe is the worst, or feel is the biggest reason for them not wanting to work in a regular job for a living. I could not count the number of people that I have spoken to that say their biggest annoyance is being accountable to someone, having a boss, or even that terribly outdated phrase 'working for the (wo)man!'. And yes there is much to be said that being treated potentially like a school child by your 'superiors' at work, or feeling under pressure to perform for an outside entity, can be very stressful and dehumanising. Lots of people have the dream of 'no boss' or becoming their own boss, and freeing themselves from the regular puppet show you and they are currently going through. This is often the 'dream' I hear people talking of, or in fact the reason people say to me how great it must be not having a boss, or someone looking down your neck all the time. You do have to be a little careful here though, because ultimately you do need that accountable body, as we have previously discussed. Being your own boss, in reality, is exactly as it says. You become that accountable body. If you leave your job and start to live your life in a more self-sustained way you very quickly find that there is nobody there to phone you up if you decide not to get out of bed in the morning. I'm guessing at the moment you would never in a million years just think of waking up, deciding it's too cold out, not bother phoning up your boss and just turning over and going back to sleep right? And even if you did, come 9.15am who do you think will be phoning you up and giving you an earful? The same person who means you wouldn't actually do it in the first place. Your accountable person! Now, don't get me wrong, there is great and powerful motivation that comes to life when you decide to live your life through your passions and for yourself. You will hopefully find as I did that as you make the step towards the different way of life, that you feel extremely motivated, excited and ready to tackle the world around you. However, there are going to be days though that will be tough, that are going to be lonely, that are going to be scary. There are going to be times where you are worried, where you are not sure what to do, and where you may start to struggle, and things just may not be going your way. This is just a reality of life. As great and powerful and fulfilling as you will find it over on this side of the fence with me, you, as I have, and I will again, will find some days that are difficult. Many new entrepreneurs and self-employed people find themselves becoming very lonely and isolated, especially to begin with, and it is critical that you begin your new life with the correct frame of mind. You *are* going to be accountable for what you do, that is the bottom line. You will no longer have the excuses we discussed to blame, the crappy boss, the other work colleagues who climbed over you to get promoted, the poor IT infrastructure…whatever it is, it will no longer exist. You and you alone are about to become the sole accountable person in your life. You are going to be the HR department, you are going to be the IT department, you are going to be both the employee and the employer. The buck is very quickly and firmly going to stop with *you*. You may find yourself coming up with new excuses and blockers around why you can't find things to do, or why you don't feel motivated today. Now despite the fact I've just scared you off with that rather overwhelming statement, I want to follow it straight up with another one…in that it is going to be ok! The attitude you must learn to adopt is that despite now being responsible for all things, you are still, after all, like me, only human. There are going to be aspects of your new life that you will have no idea about, or maybe have no experience or skills in. There are going to be days where you just don't *feel* good. And again, this is OK! Give yourself a break and don't be too harsh....be a good boss!

The next thing you can do for yourself as you venture to my side of the fence is to get yourself in the frame of mind that you are accountable for all things. This doesn't however make you immediately responsible for getting them done! You are now in charge of everything, but you *can* get support and input from anyone and everyone that you choose too. One of the biggest mistakes I made when I first made the jump was to think that I needed to physically sort everything out myself. You can't, you simply can't do it! Do not try, because all you will do is believe that you are failing at what will turn out to be an impossible job. If you need help setting up a business bank account or a limited company and don't know what you are doing.... then ask someone else to help, or pay someone to do it! 'Well, what if I don't have much money to set up my business, I can't get someone in to do everything for me?' you say. Yes, that's a very fair statement until I give you two simple scenarios:

SCENARIO 1

It's the first week you have jumped the fence and you have decided to set up as local accounting firm and on your 'to-do' list for the day are two items.

1. Go online and set up a limited company
2. Phone fifty local companies to see if you can offer them any services

You decide that obviously you need to set up your company before you can start trading as a limited company so first thing you sit down and go online and look at starting a limited company. As you haven't done it before you spend four hours surfing the internet until you finally realise you need to go to the Companies House website (this is actually where you need to go in the UK, so I've saved you some time already!) and there you can register your limited company. Once you finally get that finished you then spend the rest of the day phoning your local business list and manage to phone fifty of them, netting one job with a company that wants you to do their annual return for them. The job is worth £300.

SCENARIO 2

It's the first week you have jumped the fence and you have decided to set up an accounting firm and on your 'to-do' list for the day are two items.

1. Go online and set up a limited company
2. Phone fifty local companies to see if you can offer them any services

You decide that obviously as you don't know how to set up a limited company it may be nice to get someone to do it for you. You find a specialist online within thirty minutes of looking, you phone them up, give them all your details, pay them £99 and then leave them to it. You then spend the rest of the day phoning local businesses. You manage to phone fifty of them, netting yourself *two jobs*, one the same as in scenario 1, the other a client who has just fallen out with their accountant and wants to put you on a retainer for £300 a month.

Now this is obviously a simplified and positive outcome example, but it demonstrates perfectly the truth of working for yourself. It is well and truly possible that you were only one or two phone calls away from getting the extra job. But by being reluctant to engage others to help, or by thinking it is 'cheaper' to do it yourself, you lost out on a large amount of ongoing income for the sake of £99. The trouble is you ***don't know when this happens***, so you are oblivious in Scenario 1 that you have potentially made a poor decision. Equally there is no guarantee that Scenario 2 will happen if you do spend the £99. However, running your own business or working for yourself is ***always*** a game of numbers in one way or another, so the more often you can behave more like Scenario 2, the law of averages says you will be making the right decisions. Of course, there is a balance, you can't obviously take on staff, or pay consultants to do all your admin work from day one, that is ridiculous. But you do need to understand that it is important to make good judgement calls when it comes to deciding how to spend your time, and the reality is that spending time networking and talking to potential clients is ***always a key priority***, even more so when you first start out. Personally, I have been in the situation many times where I just decided to make one last call, or send one last email, or even submit a quick pitch for an advertised web contract online, where the complete opposite of my expectation has come to fruition. I remember pitching for one website design job on an online contract site, which was at the end of the day and I just threw my details in, said hello and offered to talk over their requirements. I ended up talking to the client a few days later and picked up I think what was probably a £300 or so web design job. This particular client then ***directly*** led me to a regular retainer from their current company, and then ***another*** regular retainer from a new company after my contact moved roles, so now I have both companies as regular clients and have earned thousands from them both over the last few years.... all from just dropping someone an email. Absolutely 100% true story, and the two companies are two of my biggest clients. Will it happen again? I hope so! Maybe not though, but if every time I push the boat out and just make that extra effort, then each and every contact is an opportunity for that to happen again.

So, as well as taking control of the day-to-day decisions on where you spend your time, I strongly recommend you also spend more of your time planning than you have before. Once more, this is purely about taking control of your environment around you and maximising your opportunity for success. I personally have got in the habit of last thing on a Sunday evening of looking at my week ahead and planning (even sometimes just on a high level) what I want to achieve the coming week. I may even break down the week into blocks of activity to achieve those results. Quick bit of advice here, get yourself a 'productivity diary'. Awesome investment. I've never been one for down to the minute micro managing and I don't think you need to either, but depending on the type of person you are (which you will know better than me!) you can do anything from a simple to do list for the week, right through to hourly slots where you assign yourself tasks. You may even want to experiment with both, to see which best suits you. This on a very simple level is another layer of that accountability that will be needed to succeed when on your own. Be honest (and brutal if necessary) with yourself at the end of the week to see what you have achieved. If it hasn't worked in your favour, try another approach. Try blocking time, try setting reminders, anything and everything to find the best and most productive way for you to achieve. Now, despite this and your best intentions, you will also find very quickly that your nicely drawn up plan will at some point be scuppered. An urgent call from a client, a cold call coming in from a potential new customer, a task that has gone pear shaped and takes twice as long as expected. So, you must be *flexible* with this planning. Even if you end up micro managing your time, there will be points where perhaps one evening you have to revisit your plan, or reprioritise your work. Don't let it affect or annoy you, this will all be part and parcel of your need to remain flexible to the needs of your customers and your business. You will eventually find your feet and what works for you. Plan to succeed, but succeed through being flexible to the changes around you.

The bottom line when it comes to your new frame of mind and ways of working is back to what I said at the beginning of this chapter. Make yourself accountable for what is going on in your life and business. Use your intuition, your skills, your experience, to ***make informed decisions*** about everything that is going on. Just remember the buck stops with you, but you do not have to carry the burden all by yourself. Not doing everything yourself isn't being a failure…. failure is not applying yourself to the best of your abilities to get the job done, regardless of who does it, when it's done, and how it gets done. Remember we discussed you will fail at things, but do not see this as a sweeping failure. Use it, learn from it and move on. That is how you will maintain motivation and take control of what is happening on a day-to-day basis.

Chapter 9. Entering your chosen market

Whether you have your secret desire, or not, this next part of the transition to success is still relevant. It is highly likely that whatever your dream is, or whatever you just first chose to do, the reality is it is in some way or another going to be a type of business. Regardless of whether you want to consult with companies, sell something, become a gardener, or brew beer, all of these are still a form of doing business. Even if you are working for yourself as self-employed (as I do) you alone are still a representation of your 'business'. You in fact, in all these scenarios *are* your business. Remember, 'you *are* your job'.

Because whatever you are going to do is going to be a business, there are two vital things that a new business needs. These are:

1. Some kind of business plan (more detail later)
2. A proof of concept

I can't count the number of times someone has come up to me and said 'I'm going to start a business that sells product/service X to person/business Y'. Yet, when I start digging in to the detail, I find out ninety-nine times out of one hundred that they haven't actually asked in detail why Y actually wants X. They have just decided for themselves it is a good idea.

For those of you who are old enough let's take a look at the Sinclair C5 electric vehicle as an example. Back in the 1980's this was probably the equivalent of now just popping out a supersonic flying car. It was *very* advanced for its time and in fact I would argue (other than aesthetically) would not be out of place if it had just rolled out on to the market today in 2022. The product was innovative, it potentially solved the problem of congestion, it was green (which back then was almost unheard of) and it was for its time a stylish piece of kit. However, it totally bombed. They only ever sold five thousand units. The reason it failed is because they neglected to do two very important things. One, they never researched and defined their market. It was marketed as an alternative for car drivers and for cyclists. Well, it turned out that neither of them were particularly interested as it never really presented itself as a viable alternative for either. Car drivers didn't like the fact it was open to the elements, while cyclists didn't like how it behaved as a heavy cumbersome bike when the battery ran out.

Sinclair had been too ambiguous and launched it as a 'catch all' for fixing everyone's' problems, which ultimately leads to nobody being particularly enamoured by it, as it never really solved anyone's problem. The other huge issues that stood against them was their marketing strategy. After a very expensive launch event the C5 didn't even become available to buy for three months. Everyone had forgotten about it! They had not targeted their marketing, they had not understood their audience and they had made the fatal mistake of just thinking that if you launch a great product, it will find its own customers and sell itself. This just doesn't happen, at any level.

These same basic principles apply to us as individual's working for ourselves, wanting to start a small business, or registering as self-employed. You may end up being the best gardener in the county, or brew the best beer you've ever tasted, but unfortunately for you, unless you do something about making sure people want what you have and do a good job of selling the concept to them, nobody is going to care. On some levels this will be very easy, as it was for my first basic web design job I did for that glorious £8. I simply sent a slightly grovely email and got the feedback I needed. It will however become more complicated as you mature your alternative working lifestyle and get involved in larger, more complex things. Now you don't have to become a salesperson as such, or get a degree in marketing. I probably dislike this side of my businesses the most and don't pretend to be an expert salesperson, but I do understand the core principles. I have a very simple system that I use that you can apply to your new way of life and that will make a huge difference to how quickly you can 'sell' yourself/idea. Once you join my side of the fence there are two core principles that I want you to think about any and every time you prospect, or talk to a potential customer, regardless of size or complexity. You need to identify your customer, find a problem they have and show as easily as possible how you can solve it….

Very simply……. they need to like you!

Point 1 here is simply about the basics of marketing and sales. Nobody will buy or pay for anything that firstly they don't even know about, and secondly, they don't perceive as something that solves a problem for them. End of. Now it may be that to you it obviously solves a problem (Sinclair C5), but if your potential customers aren't on the same page as you then you may as well give up. This is why our proof of concept is so vital when we begin our new business. We must understand ***who our customers are and what we do for them***. Now we can take the example of something in its simplest from, for instance in the situation of becoming a gardener. People have a garden that needs tending and you can tend it for them. Easy right? So, you just get yourself some tools, print some flyers and away you go. Well, no, go try that and see how long it takes to get a customer. Why? Because there are already fifty other gardeners in your area doing exactly the same thing, many of whom are established, and many of whom have clients that are extremely happy with the service, so why would they hire you!? They wouldn't. So, what do we do about it? We firstly understand the market. Spend some time reviewing and investigating every single provider doing the same thing you wish to, be it geographically if needed if it's a local service. Understand every offer that is currently available. What kind of gardening services are being marketed? How much are people charging? How many reviews do the best gardeners in your area have on their website? What media do they use to advertise? You need to become an expert on everything that is happening in your proposed market in order to understand it and in order to find your way in (people often call this 'finding a niche', but this is the only time you will hear the phrase in this book, as you know, I hate it and its vastly overused in trying to sell you social media marketing courses and other such expensive rubbish). The reason I call it a 'way in' is because you need to see it almost as a private club that has membership requirements. You need to be able to understand the club, the way it works, the big players and the customers, in order to become a member. Once you are 'in' it is much easier to progress as you understand better the world around you. For me this was first the web-design world and bidding for work on job boards. There were hundreds of registered designers on the particular site I chose and many of them had completed hundreds of contracts. From reviewing the best people on there I was able to see that those that were successful were those who had exceptional feedback. So, I thought to myself, how can I get feedback when these established people will be wining all the contracts because they already have feedback? And that is where my lucky £8 comes in. I trawled the site for the lowest paid most dull job there was and found that nobody had offered to do it! That is when I sent my email, was honest and open that I needed feedback, but told the customer that I was going to solve their problem. The rest as you now know is history.

Now once you understand your chosen market and the current offers available, you need to take the approach of understanding what the customer needs that is either not catered for, or is not being catered for well. Then you need to find the best way to tell them about it! The reality with this is you need to 'talk' to them. This is not literally stopping people in the street and asking to mow their lawn; this is using your newly acquired knowledge of the market, the ways the competition advertise and gain clients, and using those same systems to start engaging with the market. Another great and often un-tapped area when starting a new venture is friends and families. Talk to your current network of people you know. Do they have a gardener, who do they use, what do they do for them, why do they like them? What do they not do for them that your friend or family member would like from them? It is not rocket science, you just need to keep the principle of exploration in your mind and just engage, engage, engage with the market and its customers. Incidentally it will also allow you to perhaps lean on those close to you, as of course, your sister/mother/best friend will swap you out to be their gardener, however good their current one is! This can help kick start your experience for quoting jobs, gaining feedback reviews, and learn much more about the practicalities of what you are trying to do. Learn more and more about who they are and what they want. Only then can you start to understand where the gaps are, what the 'hooks' are for customers that make the current big players in the market successful. You could even go as far as working your way through every gardening service in your local area as a customer yourself. Then while they are on your property, chew their ear off with probing questions about what they do, who they work for, what kind of customers they have…and so on. Again, form my own experience as I began to understand the online web-design contract work, I found that I kept coming across people who just didn't really understand what they needed to do. Someone had decided to start a business and just posted on the board they needed a website. It would often become apparent that they didn't really know what was going to go on it, how it was going to look and how they might sell from it. So, I chose that opportunity of identifying a problem, to fill the gap. I slowly progressed from just designing pretty websites, to offering full width packages of digital consultation. I now often work with people on a much wider level, producing their site, content, graphics, stationery, marketing, etc., all because I listened to the market and developed my offer to fulfil the need.

Moving on to point 2. People need to like you. This may seem very simple, but from my own experience I would say to you that once you have your business off the ground and you ensure you have a good offer, this principle is the most powerful tool in your arsenal. If you have a great offer, you have marketed it well and have access to the customer base, and you do not build ***rapport*** with your customers, they will not use you. I have learnt over the last few years that this is a vital part to the success of my business. I would probably say, without trying to show off, that whenever I speak to a potential client for one of my businesses, I have a successful conversion rate of 90%. This is huge. But there is good reason for it. Firstly, my business offers have been honed over the last few years with clear offers to my customers, so I get good quality leads. But secondly and more importantly, I have learnt to build rapport with customers within a few minutes of speaking to them. There is no secret to it either, it's not fancy selling techniques or pressure tactics, it is simply learning to start reading your customer from the first moment you speak to them. You may well have heard of this before as being referred to as 'mirroring'. It is part of many sales techniques, but it is also a basic human habit that can be used to build very quick rapport with a stranger (customer). I will often speak to a new client first for my businesses either by phone or on a zoom call. I may have exchanged a few emails with them, but ultimately, I like to speak to them as quickly as possible so I can firm up the personal connection. The very first thing you should do regardless of who they are is to present yourself instantly with a friendly and confident greeting. Straight off the bat be enthusiastic, welcoming and direct with a smile on your face and maintain good eye contact. This will immediately disarm any anxieties or worries your customer may have about the type of person you may be. It will instantly say to them you are friendly, non-confrontational and are here to help them. Then from the moment they open their mouth in response ***pay great attention to exactly what they are saying***! Listen to their voice, their pitch, watch their facial movements and body language, listen to the types of words and phrasing they use....everything they are giving you. Then straight away start to match their 'rhythm'. Are they talking slowly, softly, or expressive and loud? Are they waving their arms around or sitting in a more relaxed posture? Do they smile as they speak, do they swear a lot, or do they maintain strong eye contact? ***Feel*** their rhythm and reflect it back to them. Show them that you understand them, that you 'get' them. Pay attention to these characteristics throughout your whole conversation with them and engage with them how they want to be engaged. This is not any kind of 'cheat' or deception, the person is ***showing*** you how they want to be engaged. They may be very animated and excited about their requirements, so will want you to be the same in order that they see you as a good fit. Some may be more reserved and focused on detail, so again show them you can be the person that gets them and can help them with their problems. They in turn will then understand you better and want to engage with you more because they will like what they see. You are not looking to deceive anyone, it is normal human behaviour. Just get in sync with them. If they are loud and enthusiastic, then bring out your own best loud and enthusiastic side. It doesn't have to be exactly the same, it just needs to be your own internal reflection of the right parts of you. Its almost like 'dressing appropriately for an occasion'.

In combination with you interacting with your potential customers in the right way, you also need to make sure you listen to what they are saying. You need to understand clearly what they want. I like to call it 'what looks good'. The 'looks good' technique is one of the very few tricks I have bought with me from my old world of Programme and Project Management. We always used it when discussing actually getting things done in large complex programmes of work. You can have as much resource or enthusiasm as you want at any level, but you will not achieve anything unless you understand what you and your customer are trying to ***actually achieve***. 'What looks good' is what will actually be left behind and completed after you have finished working on it. So, for instance, for the gardener it is specifically understanding the exact picture of the garden the customer sees once you have packed up your belongings and left them to enjoy it. Try to focus on what they see as the end desired result, and construct your questions around understanding what they want to achieve. This is basically putting your approach to the conversation into an 'outcomes' focused view. You are looking to see the distant end goal the customer is looking to achieve, then you can wrap your conversation around how your offer can provide that outcome, and build your offer so they can see *you* are the person who can realise it.

There are a million conversations we could have about building a market, client interaction and 'sales', but really that is a whole other book. What I hope I have got across is the main principles I believe you need for basic success in building a customer. Converting those leads is focusing on understanding the customer, identifying their problems or aspirations, providing a solution for that, and building basic rapport. Focus on that and you will build a solid foundation that you can then develop into your own way of doing business.

Chapter 10. JFDI!

Hopefully most of you will know what the acronym JFDI means, if not I suggest you just type it in to Google and give it a click (not at work!). A short, sharp, and to some, offensive set of letters. Yet underneath it comes a very powerful message. I have talked before about the importance of taking accountability for yourself in your new life, and this chapter is simply a follow up from that. One of the beautiful snippets of experience I can share with you from my own journey from the other side of the fence, is that on a very simple level you can get *very* far in your new life by simply doing what you said you were going to do. It was another one of those wonderful surprises that I just took as given through my life, but actually found there are *rafts* of people who do not follow through on what they say they will. You must remember a time where you have asked friends for a reliable tradesman, or recommendation for a restaurant, or perhaps somewhere to take the children? You asked because at some point you have been let down by one of the afore mentioned businesses and are looking to someone you trust who has had a good experience. How many times have you had appointments missed through your life, or had people not quite finished work for you in your job? Lots I'm sure, I know I have. This may seem crazy to you, obvious, or even in a way too basic, but I can promise you now that when you are master of your own destiny and talking to customers or clients, you (like I have) will very quickly find that a large number of people in this world simply want someone they can trust to do what they say they will. I can honestly say that probably fifty percent of my new customer base for web design has come to me because they have been let down by a previous provider. Either that, or I have completed an initial piece of work to the standard and time I said I would, and they have come back to me for more. Many of my repeat customers, through several of my business practices, have said numerous times that they like to engage with me because ***I am reliable and consistent***. I have spoken to dozens of individuals and companies that regularly tell me of difficulties they have with reliability of providers and where they have been let down by people not delivering on promises. I guess it depends on the type of person you are, but I find this insanely crazy. It makes no sense, yet I have learnt that it is rife, particularly in the world of small business and self-employment. You will be extremely surprised how by just doing this simple thing, will make a huge difference to your capability to maintain success as you move on. I have even recently had someone phone me out of the blue who said they were chatting to a friend down the pub about problems he was having with his small business and his friend said he had a friend who knew someone who had helped him a lot with his business. That's two degrees of separation! Friend of a friend, gets given my number, some random man phones me up and now I consult on three of his small businesses. All because I just did what I said I was going to do for one of his friends' friends! My only explanation is that I assume people are unable to take the accountability required to succeed in their lives. We touched on how important this was earlier, about self-accountability and 'being your own boss'. Perhaps some of these people have moved from a corporate environment and not been able to make the switch of assuming accountability for what they produce or others produce on their behalf. Or maybe if they have been self-employed forever, they have never really seen any consequences from producing poor outputs. Perhaps it is more complex than this, but it doesn't really matter. What I do know is that it is very prevalent and something that both you and I can take ***full advantage of***. If you can simply ensure that you follow through, do as you say, and produce or provide whatever you said you would on time and to quality, you will benefit from this massive advantage. There are people in all industries simply looking for trustworthy, reliable individuals to help solve their problems. As part of my work as a small business adviser I work with sectors across a huge spectrum and I can tell you that there is not a single small business that doesn't suffer from having suppliers that don't deliver. Any and every industry I have worked in, they all experience the same problem. So…..regardless of where you are going to focus your energy, you can be confident that your own potential clients or customers will have had the same problems. This JFDI approach to any scenario is all about following through on your promises. The first key point here is to make sure you *do not* promise something you can't deliver. It is very easy, certainly early on in you transition, to be compelled to be a 'yes person', or to over promise on what you can do for someone. You may find a little desperation creeping in and want to be a people pleaser, or even when you feel desperate to 'win' a certain customer. This is perfectly normal; you just need to recognise it and resist the urge to overpromise. That's not to say you can't go the extra mile. I actively encourage that, particularly at the beginning of your journey, or when working with a customer or client for the first time. Take my first website job that was worth £8 again. It took me several hours to get back up to scratch on my studying, but the customer didn't know that, nor did they need to. I was more than confident I could work in my own time to catch up on the latest programming skills in order to fix the problem, as I had done similar things years before. It may have taken an up-to-date expert five minutes, but as far as the customer knew there was no difference as this side of it is not something you need to share. Just make sure you *are* sure you can deliver. It is very important to remain grounded and understand what you can and can't do in reality. Do not get out of your depth unnecessarily just so you have a better chance of winning a customer over. You may think 'I'll sort it out' or 'I'll work out what needs to be done' but you can very quickly find yourself in hot water if it turns out to be more complex than you hoped, or even undeliverable. I had good reason and some background knowledge of my example, so I made a judgement call based on good information. This is all you can do and it is something you will need to learn from your own experience, I cannot be there every time for you. This is even more important for the further reason that in reality, you really only have one chance with someone. If you over promise and fail to deliver you will just join the long list of failed contractors or companies that they have used before, and you will likely never get to interact with them again. It is *pivotal* that you are transparent and honest at all points and are really clear on what can and can't be done. I myself many times have had to say to a potential client the word 'no'. It is not a dirty word and in fact I would say the majority of the time my clients have actually thanked me when I have been honest with them. They don't want to waste your time, or their own. It may not even be that you don't have the skill set or contacts to deliver something, I have often been in the position where I have had to say to a client that I think their desired outcome is not possible by anyone. Furthermore, in some instances I have commented I believe it is in fact not something that can be achieved. Again, in the majority of cases (maybe not immediately) I have ended up having the client come back to me and thank me for my honesty when they have eventually worked out it couldn't be done. Equally if you are not the right person for the job, or an aspect of the job, then say so. It isn't a failure to not be the right answer to a problem. It is a failure however to put yourself forward to deliver something you are unable to. Learn to get the right balance. Certainly, initially take less risk than perhaps you would once you are well established in your field. Remember as always, we are not looking to avoid failures, but we don't want to be unable to deliver on a specific task for a client or customer.

So assuming we develop the mindset for a well-rounded approach to your pitching to clients and customers, the core rest of the principles for the JFDI approach is..well..just that. Just do it! Make it happen. You have pitched for something you are clear you can deliver, and you have provided an acceptable time line and a set of deliverables that tell us 'What looks good'. That in fact is the hardest part. But if you have made sure you have done that within the parameters of honesty, you simply now just need to do it! Plan your work! Develop a basic understanding of a project management approach and then ensure you implement a ***plan for delivery***. You may feel this is not relevant to you, but I promise you now, regardless of what you are doing, whether it be cleaning houses, or creating a new piece of software for someone, the principles are the same.

1. Define your deliverables
2. Determine when you will know when they are completed (the 'what looks good' approach)
3. Put a time scale against each deliverable
4. Order your deliverables on a time line that you review regularly
5. JFDI!

Furthermore, this approach needs to be cemented in the core operations of your day-to-day activity. As well as low level planning and specific deliverables, you will also utilise this mindset for the wider and higher-level aspects of your business. Regardless of what you are doing, whether on your own, or starting a bigger business, you will have tasks that need to be completed. Some of these are administrative and some are for the wider health of the business. Tax returns, cash flow, marketing, product design, telesales, leaflet drops, and so on…..You get the idea. All of these types of wider activity are there to underpin and grow your own business or 'brand' as many call it. We discussed earlier utilising planning for your time, be it high or low level, but certainly initially you may find yourself overwhelmed by what is in front of you to do. This is ok! If you find long lists of outstanding tasks (often the ones you don't really want to do!), just simply use the JFDI. Pick one of your lists up, look at the first item and just do it. However small, or big, or scary. Just get that ticked off. If it takes you all day, or two days, then fine. Then after that go to the next item and concentrate just on getting that completed. Carry on with this process until you become less worried or feel more in control with the situation. This will again sound like common sense, but in my own experience I found it quite overwhelming at times juggling things and you can end up overthinking and not achieving anything. The exercise of just focusing on the one item can give you back the sense of control and if you need to do this for two or three items until you feel better, then this is fine. Get yourself mentally back in control and then you can start multitasking. Don't let anxiety or fear overwhelm you into inaction, just like it did when you were in your job.

Chapter 11. Reality Checks

So far, we have discussed that the core principles of everything to do with quitting work well are all actually quite simple. That's not to say they are not difficult to achieve, otherwise everyone would be writing this book having done the journey. Just because it is simple doesn't make it easy. It does make it possible though. The next topic of discussion is making the assumption we are making or have made the transition and will talk about the reality of what is to come. You will, like me, be looking to start some kind of venture or ventures, whatever they may be. When you do, you ***must*** make sure that you run them through a reality check. What do I mean by this? Well, it's great to be impassioned, motivated and work hard to build a new life outside of having a job. As I have said before, it is actually a requirement for success. And again, as before we have discussed that you will fail at some things, for which we will learn from and brush ourselves off to fight again. What we haven't discussed in detail is actually making *good business decisions* though. That is the reality check. Now, yes I have said that anyone can achieve anything they desire, within reason. And this still stands, don't be held back by thinking too big, or outside of the box. You will however, always need to make sure you apply reality to every situation you find yourself in. I mentioned in part one of the book about running for POTUS (president of the United States), which regardless of how hard I work, I simply can't achieve because we live in reality and it isn't going to happen. I could have a hundred million pounds for my campaign, but firstly I doubt even with that I could fool enough people to vote for me, and secondly to be POTUS you need to have been born in America. So, you see it is important to understand that despite you not having limitations, there *are some things that just cannot 'be'*. This works at all levels and again is a principle I use frequently and hope to pass on to you, so you can benefit from it when doing your own thing. Whenever you decide on a particular path, be it bidding for a contract, starting a whole business, buying a few things to sell on line, the basic reality check is a system that will work for any situation. It will apply whether it be a one-off output, or a fully-fledged business idea. Yes, there are many tools, articles, videos etc on how you go about building a business plan and testing the market, working out profits, determining cash flow and so on. These are all important skills to master as you mature in your journey. But there is also the base line of a few simple facts that can give you great insight into whether what you are looking to do can be achieved in a very short period. It is however, a little more art than it is science in my opinion, so I will follow with a few examples shortly. The basis for this however is the principle of covering the ***wider angle***. When working out a new business idea or pitching to a customer, you may find that you focus on the direct details in front of you. Customer X wants product/service Y, I can provide Y and can charge Z. Simple on the surface, yes? Well, how many customers do you think you will get each day/week/month? five? This is fine if you have a high value product/service to offer. Five is not good however, if you are planning to offer out your product/service at a few pounds. Equally five thousand, during any given time period is not so good if you have a low value product/service that takes a long time to deliver. Can you deliver that many? You will see what I mean by this being an art in the below examples a little more, as these questions you need to explore are all individual for every circumstance. It is difficult to simply determine basic principles to cover every eventually as there are endless opportunities for you to get involved in. I do however, have a few, for which you can start to build your own 'art' of doing reality checks and building a simple business plan.

Is it deliverable? E.g. can it be done, be it cost, time, quantity, or quality. Whatever commodities are used to produce the output, can there be a realistic and workable time frame to achieve what you need to?

Is it scaleable? Do you have a big enough market share to try to take, are you able to scale your outputs?

Is it profitable? Can it make positive financial contributions to your new way of life? Can this idea provide enough money to cover your costs from your expenditure analysis?

Do you want to do it?! It may not be a black and white answer, but realistically do you think you would enjoy what it is? Can you see yourself becoming passionate in this area, or do you realise it is a necessary stepping stone to greater things? Make sure you understand *why* you are doing it and if you really want to.

These are clearly not the full list of all you need to do, but are four powerful overarching questions that you can explore to do a quick review of whatever it is that you are looking to do. Say a 'starter business viability test' to get you thinking about what wider aspects of your new life you need to take into consideration. I will try and bring these a little further to life with two examples, one theoretical, one of my own.

Theoretically, let's say you have just decided to start your own gardening firm. You quickly have twelve clients in your home town and are slowly building a nice little business for yourself. You receive a call from someone who has been given your number as a recommendation and asks you to quote for regularly tending their garden. As you discuss a little further you find out that this person has a huge two-acre plot that will require many hours a month looking after and could double your monthly income. You then find out that they live one hundred miles away. Now, on the face of it, you think this seems pretty straight forward, you take the work, you factor in the cost of the drive and you provide the new customer with a quote in hopes they take you on. XYZ yes? And yes, you could do that. That may not be a bad decision. Or may it? Will the extra time spent travelling and the potential growth of such a large commitment early on in your business stop you from building your local, sustainable business quicker? Are you really practically going to be able drive one hundred miles three or four times a month, without delays or problems? What happens if in a few months when you have worked hard to get the grounds up to par, they then decide they can tend it for themselves so don't need you anymore? Is your exposure to this too great to risk not spending time on building your business locally? Is it safe committing yourself to one person who may let you down in the future? If you have a breakdown of your truck, can you get there still as easily as if it was just round the corner? I could drive another hundred questions to you about this, but it is pointless, and in fact if we overdo it, we would end up talking ourselves out of doing anything. The exacerbated point I am trying to make here is that you must always look at the high-level detail outside of your own commitment and capabilities. The real world that can affect everything around us. Yes, you may be desperate to take the contract in this situation and I'm not actually saying there is a right or wrong answer (the art of it) as you may decide the positives out weigh the potential negatives for your particular circumstances at that particular time. What I am saying though is that for all business decisions, large or small, you ***must look at the bigger picture*** as to what can happen. It is not just as simple as a high-ticket gardening contract. There are external factors and influences that you must consider, as well as its impact on the rest of your business.

For my second example I am going to talk about table crystals. What? What the hell are table crystals you ask? Well, they are the cute little plastic fake-coloured diamonds that people put on tables at weddings and end up in children's mouths, or up their noses. A bizarre example yes, but I use it for a reason as it was one of my very first business ventures, I tried about fifteen years ago, that started well and seemed to have a lot of potential. For our own wedding my wife had very much enjoyed buying all the little bits and bobs for the table themes and found that she had seen some table crystals in a magazine that she could not find anywhere. Light bulb! Gap in the market! So, we tracked down a supplier in the Far East, got samples, prices etc and began to sell little bags of crystals online on eBay for I think £3.99 to £5.99 depending on volume and size of crystal. Started with good profit margins too of around 60%. So, we trundled along for about two or three months and found that we were starting to sell *lots* of these crystals. We were both working at the time in jobs, so we were fulfilling these orders in the evenings and taking them in sacks down to the sorting office. It got to the point where we were doing anywhere up to fifty plus orders a day. It was taking us three hours per night to do, but we had huge sacks to take to the post office. As time progressed postage prices increased a little, other people started selling them, we dropped our price a little, but merrily carried on as we had so many orders. After about eighteen months it was starting to get to the point where it was too big to manage as just a side hustle. So, I crunched a few numbers to see where to go from there. By the time I had factored in the changes in post, the cost of the envelope, the stickers for addresses, the printer, the eBay fees, I worked out that we were making less than 50p per sale. It suddenly dawned on me that two people were busting their rear ends every night after work, just to make an extra £25! And this was before taking into account time, driving to the post office, stock investment etc etc. We had thought we were so busy and doing so well that we could go full time, but the reality of the situation is that the market had changes, there was more competition, increasing costs and erosion of our profits. Even if one of us was to quit and do it full time it was an ever-decreasing erosion of sustainability for the business. A friend of mine who unfortunately is now no longer with us, used to have a great saying that fits well in this situation. 'Don't be a busy fool. Turnover for show, profits for a pro'. A bit East End like I know sorry. But the upshot is just because something can keep you busy and or is popular, or feels like it is going well, it does not in reality make it a good business. We had worked incredibly hard to build our small business at the time, but the reality was the market had developed and there was no sustainability in there anymore. Perhaps if we had 'doubled down' and flooded the market we may have got enough of a share to make it work, I don't know. You just have to make decisions at any point with the information you have. Again, no definite right or wrong answer here, but in this situation we decided to call it a day.

It goes to show that not just at the beginning of a business do you need to ensure you are being realistic; the world is in constant flux and things change so be ever vigilant with where you are putting your efforts to use. Make sure you do not make business decisions that seem straight forward in the short term, but may damage your growth in the long. And always remember to review constantly your business efforts to ensure that they are able to withstand changes to the world around them, or to determine perhaps that their time has come to an end, and move on to focus elsewhere.

The reason I have referenced this as an art can hopefully be seen by the slight ambiguity of the questions posed in the first example. There is no clear ***right*** or ***wrong*** answer to either of them, and in reality, you could make both work potentially either way. It doesn't make them invalid questions, just because they are not direct and to the point. That is the point! The 'art' of it all. This again is an area you will need to develop yourself but hopefully my list of simple questions and running through my examples, will give you a baseline starting ground. The success of developing this art can only truly come with experience, much like riding the bike, and will bring with it some failures. This is normal and you will need to allow it to happen. It is how you will grow and develop your own business sense. If in doubt, or you feel you are stopping yourself from making decisions by over thinking, simply use just the base questions and give them a yes or no answer, and the majority rule wins. It's as simple as I can give you to start yourself off.

Chapter 12. What's setting out on your own / going solo actually like?

Having been in this lifestyle now for coming up to six years, it is now a topic I feel I have a pretty decent authority on. I often get asked what it is really like when discussing what I do with people, so I thought it worthwhile sharing with you the realities and experiences of living life this way. The reality is, despite all of the discussions and planning we have talked about in this book, many people just simply want to understand how it *feels*, and what it is really like living your life so differently. So, let's talk a little about my general experiences of the last years, and how it has developed me and changed me as a perso hopefully giving you some insight into how it could be for you after making the jump.

Now remember I always said that everybody's journey is different, unique and individual to them. Yet we know there are themes and similarities because of our mantras. So, my reality now, is more than possible something you yourself could experience in your own way. Firstly, I think I would say, as would most people that know me, the most profound thing that has changed in me is my ***general level of happiness***. It's a little difficult to define or quantify, but I know my wife and my parents both have seen very positive changes in my general demeanour over the last few years. I would say that I definitely feel more content with my life. I have never been what I would call a particularly positive or optimistic person, but I genuinely think I am polls apart from where I used to be. Looking back now on when I used to work in a job, I can almost hardly remember what it was like. But the few snippets I have that come forward to me, tend to be ones of a very anxious and unhappy time for me. I think I take for granted now how different it is. I remember there being a real weight on my shoulders all of the time when I was working in my job. The same anxiety and fear that comes for many of us when we are trapped in the cycle of work and reward. I simply don't have that any more. I have to pinch myself sometimes with knowing the element of freedom I have now. Strangely though I would say this freedom does not feel altogether new and has somehow felt that it has always been there with me, yet perhaps wasn't at the forefront. It can be very hard to describe, but I no longer feel those feelings of concern or anxiety over what others think of me, or if I'm going to be able to get more work and pay my bills. I think this is because I now *know* that there is a sustainable life on this side of the fence and I *know* that I am a capable person who can take charge of their own life. I *know* that if I work hard, open myself up to ideas and to the good people around me, that everything is ultimately going to be OK. Of course, I still have the same normal levels of life's ups and downs and worry about normal things, like anyone else does. I continue to have some fairly significant health issues, I have aging parents, I have a child to care for and worry about. These are all normal things though. What I don't have now is that underlying feeling of constant doubt in myself and my self-worth. There is definitely an element of self-belief that has grown stronger over the last few years, and I believe still hopefully has a long way to go yet still. I have said before that I have an anxious background and struggle socially, but I have found that living my life this new way has helped me greatly in liking myself more and feeling I have more to offer. This in turn has helped with these anxieties and fears and also how I present myself to the world. I am still more of a wall flower than an extrovert, but I feel much less judged and more comfortable with who I am, and this can make it often much easier in social situations. Yes, I'm no social butterfly and accept that I never will be, but I have definitely made progress and am able to mix better as my authentic self. I have not fundamentally changed as a person, but I do strongly believe, as I'm sure my loved ones will agree, that what it has done for me is change the 'weighting' of my personality aspects. The more negative, self-destructive traits have become weaker, while the more positive and pro-active aspects of my personality have begun to flourish. I can only put that down to living life now in this way that suits me.

'Work' wise, despite finding my initial feet quickly in the first few months, it took me a year or so to really get to grips with finding the aspects of things that I enjoy most. Even now I would suggest I have much to learn about myself and what I am capable of, and further believe it is never a journey I will truly finish. I think to some extent you are lucky that I was never one of those people who always had a dream, or knew exactly what gave them passion in their life. I think these people are extremely lucky, but if I had been one, I think it may have been a bit harder to try and 'sell you this story'. I have enjoyed everything I have done in the last few years since quitting my job, but there is definitely a maturation of the experience as time goes on, that has allowed me to hone the areas of most interest to me. This I'm sure will also happen for those of you who are worrying about not having clear direction at this point in what you want to do. I also still have the passion for new things. Even today while writing this chapter I have spent an hour this morning looking at a potential new area that I might want to start working in. Another hands-on practical skill which I may want to develop and bring in to the fold of the things I do. For me I think this really is something that you could argue is one of the 'secrets' when making this change. It truly is the thing that is most exciting when in this situation. I never really know what's going on or what's going to happen! And yes, sometimes this can be a little scary and cause anxiety, but oddly enough, never as much as I had when I had a steady and reliable job and there was less change! I think it is because I now know that I can genuinely do something about it. I have my freedom, I have my passion and I have my capability. I now **know** that these three tools are endlessly powerful and all I truly need to succeed in whatever I wish. I am not tied down to a set of rules and regulations dictated by a third party. ***I am just me and what I choose to do***. That's why it is exciting when I look at new ideas. I know that should I choose to begin a new venture or learn a new skill, that there is nothing standing in my way and I can simply do it. For so many years I used to see the fake barriers and veils of fear that would stop me in my tracks, but now I simply don't have them anymore. I'm not saying I never get scared or worried about things like money, or work coming in, or any other normal thing that people worry about. I would be lying and I'm just not doing that. Feelings like that are not ever going to go away fully and I'm not going to pretend that for you they will. Yet what I can say is it is much more measured in how I feel about it, and more importantly I genuinely believe that I have the power within me to do something about it. I know that if I stop enjoying something that I am doing, or if changes in the world around me mean I am unable to do some of it, I will be able to make changes and try something else. I have made the full transition away from the job hamster wheel and am at a junction in my life where I am genuinely OK with not having full control over everything around me. It's never going to happen! But I do have enough control to ensure I can ride anything through this journey. That, I think, is the other 'secret' that I have learnt in these past years. Things are never going to be perfect in any job, or any other situation. However, by taking control of myself, my contributions, and using my passion to drive my life, there is little I believe that I can't achieve. I strongly believe that all these feelings, experiences and principles, are also here waiting for any other person who wants to come along and join me.

I now find myself living in a world of continues flux, but it feels like one I have a good degree of control over. I have got used to living more medium and long term financially, as well as being ok with not knowing what may be coming my way today.

More than that…I have actually grown to like the fact I don't know. I know many of you will be resistant to change and perhaps afraid of it. I can genuinely tell you I was very much this way while working a job. Yet again I keep saying through this whole book, I am living proof it is possible for a regular middle aged, 'successful' person to just decide to do it differently. I did it without *any* help or guidance from someone. I would say that money now has also taken a very different role in my life. I no longer use that as a measure of who I am as a person. It no longer hangs there as the monthly 'value' others place on me. I have said before that with passion and commitment comes reward and I stand by that fully, as my life is a true testament to that. I do have more financial freedom, but I had to work hard for it and will have to continue to do so. Ironically if I think back to the questions we discussed of 'how much money would I need to quit work?' The answer for me I recall was around £50k. That was my so-called 'magic number'. I thought all my hopes and dreams would be answered and everything would slot into place if I could just get that, then quit my job, start a business…blah..blah…blah. I look back now and I know that if I had waited to get there I would never be here today, as I wouldn't have made the change. This is further cemented by the fact I have achieved that marker financially, and more, and it hasn't changed me at all, or how I feel. Somehow, I managed to get the courage I needed to make that change without it, and boy am I glad I did. What else had changed and what else does it feel like to be here on the other side? It feels like it is O…K to be in this place!!! I am not frightened of it. It will not hurt you, it will not destroy your life. And that is because you can learn as I have that these things are all actually within you. Your emotional relationships, your feelings, your 'home'. It is you and those around you. I am lucky enough to still have the house that I had when I was successfully working in my career. For this I am grateful yes, but if I had had to sell it and move, looking back now would I have regretted it and changed my mind and stuck with my job? I The genuine truth, no…. never. I am resourceful, flexible to change, focused and I work hard to achieve what I want to achieve. I do this for myself, for my family and I am happy to help you do it too. There is so much more value that is not measurable with this way of life, for those who are struggling with the everyday 'norm' or working a job. It is difficult to get here, I have already said that, and if it was easy then you would have done it already. ***But it is waiting for you. I am waiting for you. And it is worth it!***

Chapter 13. What if you just don't do it?

As we begin to close our discussion, I ask you the question What is your other option? We have talked in detail about how, like I was, you are one of those people who is basically miserable in what they are doing. Otherwise, you still wouldn't be here, yes? So, the question is a pertinent one. What are your other options? Your basic alternative option is *to stay in a job*. This is what you have been doing for x number of years so far, so you can stay where you are or even maybe look for another job. So perhaps what do you think will be different then? If you stay doing your current job, having been it for however long, unhappy, unfulfilled, fearful, and so on…. *how will things* change? Will you suddenly get happier in your current situation, or will your manager suddenly realise what you do and get you two extra staff members to help you, make you a senior manager and give you a 200% pay rise? The answer is no. Equally, even if you do, and like me you eventually get to where you think you belong, and are promoted into a high-powered job, surely its better then? No! In fact, from my own experience, it was worse. ***more pressure, more consumption, more fear, more doubt.*** Things haven't got better yet for you and I'm sorry to say it is unlikely that it ever will if you don't take action.

I was a real pro at this mind set and very much of the opinion in my job of 'it will better when'. It will be better when I get my next promotion, it will be better when I get my next pay rise. It will be better when my son is older, it will be better when that giant idiot director moves on to other things. You I am sure, will also have a whole list of 'better when' which you will be using as your current excuses for having stayed where you are. Yet if I ask you to be honest with yourself are some of these, or even all of them self-replicating? And by this, I mean, have you changed the goal posts? Did it used to be 'better when I will earn over £20k', and now perhaps it has morphed into 'better when I will earn over £30k'. This takes us right back to basics of your subconscious giving us the way out, or the reason behind why you are not making the move. We need to discuss the fact that this in not going to change unless you ***make*** it change. The fact that you feel how you feel and want for what you want, is a sign that you are needing this change. Yes, we know it is scary and harbours some challenges, some risk, some doubt.... but we have just this one life. I'm not going to get all spiritual or anything on you, but you must be generally in agreement that for this life we have right here, right now, we are only doing a one-way trip! Whether you believe in afterlife, reincarnation, spirituality, whatever…it doesn't matter. This life is this life only. So, if you are not going to make changes to make it better then you will have to just carry on as is. Carry on being anxious, stressed, miserable, full of self-doubt…rewarding your monthly cycle with some 'stuff'. It will continue if you let it. There is no rainbow at the end of fifty years of working called 'blissful retirement'; there is no knight in shining armour who is going to come and get you and take you away from it all. It's just you. Now of course people like myself can help you and guide you, but as I have said many times before, this is your journey. I cannot jump out of the plane for you!

Think of your current situation and all the things about it that have come to the foreground through our discussions here. The way your job or career has impacted your mental and physical health, your self-respect, your relationships with friends and family. It can have massive impacts on all aspects of your life. If it does, then why on earth would you not do something about it? Are we going to sit here and say that we are going to sell your health, happiness and personal fulfilment for money? For £20k, £30k, £50k, £150k. It doesn't matter. ***That is the price*** you currently hold against your own happiness and leading a better life. It doesn't matter that you have concerns about how you will cope, or what if you fail, or what if I regret leaving it all behind. Why? Because you already know deep down that you are in the wrong place, otherwise we wouldn't still be having this conversation! You have answered all your own questions and concerns by working through this with me, you just need to realise that's what you have done. You *want* to do it. ***So do it!***

I have said before and will say to anyone until I'm blue in the face that I have done it. I am not special. So 'If I have done it'..yes, you know what mantra to say! Things are not going to change for you unless you make a change. The chances of your finding 'happiness' from your next promotion, or your next pay rise are basically zero. Your mind and body is longing for a better way of doing things, to be based on your passion, your creativity, your drive. Not to slowly bore yourself to death with Quarterly Business Reports! You know your mind and body wants this now, so can you imagine what you will be able to achieve once you are impassioned, motivated and free to create? I can 99% guarantee that with hard work and passion that you can create a new life for yourself, as much as I can 99% guarantee you are waiting around for happiness and fulfilment at the moment that is never going to show up. Ok, so there is perhaps the one in one hundred people who make the move and find it was not right for them, or struggle to make the adjustment. These people are unprepared, unsure and have perhaps not worked as hard as they needed to. I have never said it is going to be a walk in the park. I have said you are ***going to have to work hard***, harder than you ever have but for one hell of a good reason. You will work to better your life, to better your health, to better your relationships. To better everything.

So, your options are simple. Take a one in hundred chance that you may find happiness carrying on in your career or job. ***Or*** take a ninety-nine in a hundred chance that there is a better life for you on this side of the fence, which will bring magic into your life and those around you. Oversimplified? Perhaps. But True? For sure.

It's getting now to the point where we have to say goodbye (for now). I have given you my insights on most things related to making the jump, and I hope I have stirred some fire within you to understand that this change has to come *from within you*. We know this life is not for everyone; many people love their job or their career, or are happy just breezing along. But, you should have enough insight now to know whether or not, like me, that is not how your cloth has been cut. It doesn't make us strange; it doesn't make us reckless, or destined to be outsiders. It makes us, us. It makes us people who need to listen to ourselves and realise that we are living our lives the wrong way. That inaction will cause repetition in our negativity and self-doubt. Remember, by just taking that *one last breath*, and *one single step* off the side of the plane, you can have the craziest, wildest, fun filled ride you could ever dream of!

Be strong my friend, take that final leap….work hard and I'll see you on the other side.

No, I haven't forgotten my promise! If you want me, just search me up and drop me a line!

Printed in Great Britain
by Amazon